WOVEN *for* PURPOSE

HOW DESIGN, BUSINESS, AND HEART CAN STITCH A BETTER WORLD

By Lily Kanter

Woven For Purpose:
How Design, Business, and Heart Can Stitch a Better World

Copyright © Lily Kanter (2026)

ISBN Paperback: 979-8-89576-198-4
ISBN Hardback: 979-8-89576-199-1

Published by:

Dedication

To my great-grandparents, Lillian and David Kanter, whose courage and foresight brought our family to America, and to my children, Max, Zeke, and Nate, may you carry forward a life and legacy guided by integrity, love, and purpose.

Table of Contents

Foreword

Most people think meaning is what you find after the struggle is over. The data says otherwise.

In a set of studies, my colleagues (Baumeister, Vohs, Garbinsky) and I studied the difference between a happy life and a meaningful one, and what we found is that they are not the same thing—and in some ways, they work against each other.

Happiness is about comfort, ease, having your needs met. Meaning comes from giving of yourself, from engaging with difficulty rather than avoiding it, from standing for something beyond your own wants. The people in our study who reported the deepest meaning also reported more stress, more worry, more time sitting with hard experiences. They were not having an easier time. They were having a more purposeful one.

Fredrickson and Cole found a similar pattern in the body. At the level of gene expression, people who were happy but lacked meaning showed the same biological profile as people under chronic threat—elevated inflammation, weakened immunity. People who had meaning, even with more stress, showed the opposite.

Meaning is not a feeling. It is a biological state.

I kept thinking about this while reading Lily Kanter's book.

Lily built Serena & Lily from a baby store in Mill Valley with a newborn in a sling. The day after her second son was born, she left the hospital, stopped by the store, found a designer's portfolio on the counter, and called her immediately. That call became a company. And this book is the honest, funny, often raw story of what it took—raising three boys while navigating investors who patted her on the head and called her "girl," surviving a lawsuit from her own board, and eventually walking away from the thing she'd spent thirteen years building because she knew it needed to become something she could no longer lead.

She doesn't call any of this sacrifice. She calls it purpose. And the data says her body knew the difference.

But what carries Lily through this story is not purpose alone. It is people.

The Harvard Study of Adult Development—85 years of data— keeps landing on the same finding: the quality of your close relationships predicts how long and how well you live more powerfully than wealth, IQ, or genetics. Isolation carries a mortality risk comparable to smoking. People with strong social ties have a 50% greater likelihood of survival.

Lily built her life around this before she ever saw the research. Shabbat dinners every Friday, phones off the table. Thirty-seven friends and family who funded her company in 17 days when it was days from going under. A best friend who, on their first coffee, proposed they skip the getting-to-know-you phase and just agree to be lifelong friends because she needed to check it off her list. The research calls this social integration—one of the strongest predictors of health and survival. Lily would just call it her life.

And then there is joy.

Fredrickson's research shows that genuine positive emotions - delight, laughter, awe—expand cognitive capacity by up to 30%, strengthen bonds, and speed recovery from adversity. Joy is not the break from meaningful work - it is what makes meaningful work possible. When Lily describes washing her hair with toothpaste in the Namibian desert while her teenage son rinsed it out with cold water, or dressing up as her co-founder for the office Halloween runway—those aren't the light moments between the real ones. The light moments are the real ones. Purpose without laughter is just endurance. Together, they become meaning.

Lily's life has changed shape many times. Corporate career to startup founder. CEO to the woman who knew it was time to hand over the keys. A business collapsing during a pandemic and opening unexpected space to sit with her dying mother in her final months. A move to Hawaii. A return to textiles and artisan craft that had been calling her for years.

At every turn, she chose what felt true over what looked impressive.

What the research keeps pointing to—and what Lily's life keeps demonstrating—is what I would call a beautiful life. Not beautiful because it is easy or pretty. Beautiful because it is built on what actually sustains a human being: purpose that costs you something, people who show up when it matters, joy you build into the everyday rather than wait for at the end, and the willingness to let your life change shape when it needs to.

A beautiful life is what feels true to you. What lights you up. What animates your soul. It is not a destination. It is the practice of choosing, again and again, what matters.

The research is clear: a life built on purpose, people, and joy is not just more meaningful. It lasts longer. This is a book about how to build a beautiful one.

Jennifer Aaker

Jennifer Aaker | General Atlantic Professor | Stanford GSB

On Repairing the World

"It is not your responsibility to finish the work, but neither are you at liberty to neglect it."
—Pirkei Avot 2:16

The concept of "repairing the world" is often discussed. Sometimes it inspires; other times it feels like someone handed you a glue stick and said, "Okay, fix humanity." It can make you feel small, or worse, helpless. In business, we'd call that "boiling the ocean," a polite way of saying, "Good luck with that."

And yet, I don't think that gets us off the hook.

I think each of us is here for a reason: not to fix everything, but to fix something. To leave the world just a little bit better than we found it, even if the ocean stays un-boiled.

Our real job in life is to figure out how. What lights us up? What are we naturally good at (besides worrying at 3 a.m.)? And how can we use those gifts to make a positive difference?

Science even backs this up. People who live with purpose and help others tend to have less anxiety, fewer physical ailments, and, according to one Northwestern University study, a 58% lower risk of death. Apparently, purpose is cheaper than supplements and more effective than therapy. Even after adjusting for money, exercise, and lifestyle, people with purpose still lived longer. So yes, doing good is also good for you.

When the Big Questions Begin

These questions tend to pop up at certain times in life when maybe a tragedy arrives at your doorstep, you're considering a new path, building something from scratch, or wondering if your life still aligns with your values. Sometimes you're lucky enough to reach a time where you have stability: a good home life, education, maybe financial success. And then, often in the quiet moments between emails and laundry, you start asking yourself:

- How did I get here?
- What were the real ingredients of my success, and can I share them with someone else?
- What is my purpose now that I have the privilege of asking this question?

But you don't have to have "arrived" to ask these questions. Most of us ask them while we're still in the chaos of balancing work and family, trying to make payroll or pack lunches, wondering how to do it all without losing ourselves along the way.

I know that tension intimately. As the co-founder of Serena & Lily, I built a company from the ground up while raising three boys. I've juggled investor meetings and school plays, boardrooms and bedtime stories. I've wrestled with ambition and motherhood, as well as purpose and exhaustion. I've swum in those choppy waters, and I know how lonely they can feel.

That's why I wrote this book.

Who This Book Is For:

This is for anyone building something meaningful without abandoning the people (or parts of themselves) that matter most. It's for:

- Parents juggling work and life balance.
- People working 40+ hours a week and wondering, "Why am I on this treadmill?"
- Entrepreneurs building companies.
- Young people trying to figure out what to do with their careers.
- Leaders who want to create cultures of purpose.
- Anyone who wants their work and life to stand for something without burning out in the process.
- And yes, anyone who wants the real founding story of Serena & Lily, including the parts that never made it to a glossy magazine.

Throughout this book, you'll find personal stories, hard-earned lessons, and practical tools. Not perfection. Not theory. Just the real, human work of building a life of purpose at home, in business, and in the world.

So, if you're ready to begin, not to boil the ocean, but to warm your corner of it, turn the page.

CHAPTER 1

How My Past Paved My Future

"Your childhood is the foundation on which your life stands. Every brick, love, struggle, joy, and pain, builds who you become."
—Oprah Winfrey

When you think about the challenges of balancing entrepreneurship and parenthood, it feels impossible. Building a business, navigating a corporate career, or creating a team culture that truly supports working parents asks the same questions: how do you stay true to your values under pressure, and how do you create something meaningful without losing yourself in the process? The challenge is real, and the rewards are extraordinary.

I've been there. I've felt the stress of trying to have it all and the fear of falling short in both roles. I've wrestled with boundaries between work and family, especially when working from home. I've felt the isolation of trying to explain founder problems to people who can't completely understand how stressful it really is to build a company from the ground up.

Before I share strategies, I want to share where I came from. Where we come from often shapes where we are headed.

I am often asked the same interview questions: "When did your entrepreneurial journey start? Tell me about little Lily."

I think I was born with the entrepreneurial itch. That itch grew into a passion as creativity and problem-solving became my fuel. The people in my life instilled core values that became my toolkit:

- Work ethic and perseverance
- Balancing structure with family priorities
- Financial acumen and self-reliance
- An affinity for numbers
- The importance of financial independence
- Innovation and problem-solving
- Finding creative shortcuts
- Spotting and creating opportunities
- Networking and relationship building
- Positive work culture
- Mentorship
- Seizing the moment
- Personal growth and intuition
- Trusting my instincts
- Continuous learning and adaptability

Those traits nurtured early became invaluable as an entrepreneur and a parent. Each experience laid foundation stones for future success.

The Childhood Entrepreneurial Spark

My brother Herman, and yes, we were teased for being named after the Munsters, we ran elaborate pretend enterprises. Drive-thru banks, talk radio shows, stuffed animal schools, and hospitals. Border Patrol even stamped the passports of our stuffed animals. It was a thriving economy with a highly flexible banking system. It went beyond the lemonade stand. I set up a basement roller rink with a snack bar stocked with candy, drinks, and popcorn. It felt fun, but it was also a form of training. Imagining scenarios, creating systems, thinking outside the box.

I grew up in a middle-class neighborhood in Kansas City, Missouri, and here I am with my cat, Smokey, around 1970.

As parents, we worry about the impact of screens. My experience leads me to wonder if less technology fosters more creativity and calm. I don't recall a youth mental health crisis on our block, just bikes and balmy nights listening to the sound of cicadas and catching fireflies. That early problem-solving became indispensable later.

My parents have shaped my work ethic, values, and sense of independence. My mother taught in a tough public school. She cared deeply, and she showed up with patience day after day. My father was a doctor for corporations; his family meant so much to him that he wanted an 8-5 schedule and did not want to be on call after hours. For years, he was the in-house physician for the General Motors factory, and we would get a new car every 3,000 miles, and our parents would drive us all over the United States on very long road trips. In 1976, my father insisted we drive to Washington DC and Valley Forge, Pennsylvania, in honor of the bicentennial on July 4th, 1976. My father then transferred to Trans World Airlines (TWA) as the Medical Director, which meant we flew standby all over the world for free. Because we flew standby all over the world, our parents had to put us on flights by ourselves because sometimes there was only one seat available. I recall getting stranded for four days at fourteen years old in Rome after they put me on a flight that needed to return to the airport due to a mechanical problem, and not being able to get on another flight for many days, but our parents never sweated it. They saw it as a way to build independence. Later, my father ran the Public Health Department, also known as the Free Clinic. I don't recall a day he missed work. Both parents left early, so my brother and I learned to get ourselves out the door. I recall dear Bev, the school bus driver with the beehive hairdo, honking to wake me up, and she would literally wait for five minutes as I got my act together and raced out the door. Come to think of it, maybe that's why I can get ready to go in five minutes.

Here I am on our Bicentennial road trip across the USA.

My parents were also tireless community volunteers. They ran organizations, and we were drafted as helpers. Many holidays, I gift-wrapped for nonprofits or volunteered at the hospital on Christmas Day. That exposure to service taught me that impact reaches beyond a paycheck.

There was no helicopter parenting. We were expected to figure things out on our own. That came in handy when I started working at twelve.

My childhood best friend, Cara Lee Krashin, and I passed out flyers in the neighborhood to advertise our babysitting services. I landed a steady job watching three little boys from middle school through high school. At fourteen, both Cara Lee and I got jobs as servers at Saddle & Sirloin, an equestrian country club on the Kansas side. Because of Blue Laws, it was BYOB, which is how a fourteen-year-old could legally be a server.

At fifteen, I moved to gift wrapping at Jack Henry, a fine men's store on the Country Club Plaza in Kansas City, Missouri. They kept me after the holidays and rotated me through departments. I worked in credit, reviewing accounts, then transitioned to sales auditing, where I counted cash, balanced daily revenue, and prepared journal entries for cash, credit, revenue, and sales tax.

By sixteen, the accounting work felt natural even when I walked days' cash deposits to the bank in a paper bag. Saturdays could be more than five thousand dollars in cash. My mother was horrified.

Here I am with Cara Lee around the time of kindergarten.

That early independence and problem-solving would later serve me well when life became a juggling act of founder calls and family dinners. At home, we had rituals that created structure. Nightly family dinners. Eating out once or twice a week. Sabbath dinner on Friday with our grandparents. We lit candles and said blessings over wine and challah. Those routines taught me that priorities need a rigid schedule. In the busiest times, you still protect what matters. Structure and flexibility can coexist. My parents made Friday night dinner a non-negotiable, but allowed me to go to the roller rink afterwards, which was a great passion in those years. That lesson became a cornerstone of how I lead and parent.

My grandparents' story added another layer. They immigrated at the turn of the century. My grandfather arrived at sixteen with his uncle and never saw their parents again. Most of the family was later wiped out in World War II by the Nazis and their collaborators. In New York, he saw ads for land grants out West and crop picking jobs in Missouri and Kansas. He had family in Joplin, Missouri, so he went to meet his cousins. They were from the same village in the Austrian-Hungarian Empire, a town called Otynia, which is now part of Ukraine, and he eventually married one of their daughters.

As a child, their stories always felt like scenes out of *Fiddler on the Roof*, filled with grit, humor, and survival. My grandparents were tireless entrepreneurs who weathered more ups and downs than I could count. Prohibition wiped out their beer company. Other ventures rose and fell, but they never stopped starting over.

I grew up wandering my grandfather's felt factory, a maze of ladders, dusty floors, and secret rooms tucked between diners and colorful neighborhood characters. What sticks with me most is not the machinery but the man behind it. Even in his eighties, I watched him stuff felt into burlap bags, his hands steady and always a smile on his face, with a desire to work until the day he passed away. That generation did not know how to quit. They built, rebuilt, and kept going, no matter how many times life reset the board.

I share these details because they are part of me. Children may not seem to listen, but they are always watching. The old country stories shaped my imagination and my standards.

Our large Kanter family always got together regularly; it was like a scene out of an immigrant sitcom. Thanks to my very close first cousin, Elissa, they still gather once a month. I have worked hard to recreate that deep sense of family and community, even though I am now 1,800 miles away from my hometown.

Our family traditions go back to the old country. This was my grandmother's family with my father on her lap around the year 1940.

My adorable parents and brother. This photo captures the joy
my parents brought to the world.

Here is my brother and me with our sweet "Papa" at a family Seder.

This is me with my dear grandmother, "Nana."

Shortcuts and Superpowers

In school, I was primarily interested in social life. Traditional classrooms bored me, which led me to one of my lifelong superpowers: clever shortcuts, now commonly referred to as "life hacks." I subscribed early to "Fake It Until You Make It." Applied math came easily; geometry did not. Proof theorems made no sense to me. Looking back, it might have been boredom more than ability. Those life hacks turned out to be priceless in the end. In entrepreneurship and parenting, you often need creative solutions, and sometimes you need to project confidence while you are still figuring it all out.

I was an honor roll student pretty much my entire life. I was the teenage daughter from hell and not the easiest teenager for my parents to deal with, but I delivered good grades, which seemed to allow them to ignore all the other insanity of being a pain-in-the-butt teenager.

Not every class required a shortcut. Junior year accounting felt like a natural-born skill. We did a project called Camper's Cove. A binder of source documents, manual journal entries into the general ledger, followed by an income statement and balance sheet, which were due in four to six weeks. I turned it in a few days. I couldn't let it go until it was done. My teacher told me to major in accounting in college.

That affinity for numbers would become a quiet superpower in business and at home. As high school ended, I was ready for the next chapter. Independence, decisions, and making my own path were about to get very real.

Defying Expectations

I applied to Arizona State at the start of my senior year, was accepted mid-year, and left high school to start college mid-year. I was ready to start adult life.

I paid my way through school with Pell grants, guaranteed student loans, and steady work. It built on my work ethic and taught financial resilience. Entrepreneurship loves both.

College in those days was very affordable. I'm still unclear how it went from less than $1,000 a year to $50,000+. I was in college a while ago, but not 100 years ago.

My parents were not thrilled about Arizona State University (ASU). Given my grades, they wanted me to attend an Ivy League school. I had been dating my on-again, off-again boyfriend, Chris Michelson, since eighth grade, so yes, I followed him. In full seventeen-year-old certainty, I told my parents that all schools use the same textbooks and that you get out of education what you put into it. Success does not hinge on a name over the door. Teenage me was very sure. I was not entirely wrong.

Choosing ASU taught me to trust my instincts even when they did not match expectations. That confidence has helped me in both my business and personal life. My younger self would love to say, "I told you so," since that choice set me on the path I am on today.

I do believe success is a fire in your belly, or it's not, and if it's a burning desire, then you figure it out. I also sometimes ask myself if my success was a way to prove that academic pedigree has no correlation. I also happen to believe that nowadays ASU is a very impressive University with very impressive programs.

I was ambitious and wanted to be a Certified Public Accountant (CPA), but life had its own lesson plan.

After a year or two of living with my boyfriend, Chris, and his childhood friend, Todd Greenberg, was too dramatic. I needed a new place, which led to a chance encounter at the apartment pool at the Cedars in Tempe. I overheard two girls talking about Kansas City. They had transferred from Kansas University. One was Elyce Cox, the other was Katy Brosnahan. I vaguely knew Katy's sister, Eve, from my Jack Henry days in Kansas City.

We became fast friends. I basically lived in their apartment. The following year, Eve moved to Arizona, and Eve, Elyce, and I got a place together. Elyce drove the beverage cart at the Biltmore Golf Course, which provided great training in service and hustle. Katy, always fashion-forward, worked at John's, a preppy clothing store. She met Andy Spade there. They clicked immediately. When an employee named Mike Carter left in 1984 to open his own men's store at 44th and Camelback, Katy and Andy followed to help him launch it. None of us knew we were watching the first chapters of a fashion empire. My friend Katy Brosnahan later became Kate Spade, co-founder of the brand that bears her name. Our other roommate, Elyce Cox (Arons), is also an early co-founder of Kate Spade and now Francis Valentine.

May Kate rest in peace. Her passing in 2018 was a profound loss, and her entrepreneurial legacy continues to inspire.

I became the bookkeeper at Carter's. The office was located on a second-floor loft, offering me a view of the action below. Carter had a unique approach to networking. He would tell certain clients there was a talented young Jewish bookkeeper upstairs and ask if they wanted to meet her. It was awkward then. With perspective, I see his intent. He cared about our futures and treated us like family. That was my first experience with a business that felt like a community, a principle I later built into my own companies.

That shop was my first taste of a startup. I learned the importance of culture, mentorship, and how small beginnings can lead to big outcomes. From that little retail job came four major consumer brands. Not bad for a 1,200-square-foot high-end specialty clothing store in Phoenix, Arizona, at 44th and Camelback.

A holiday photo shoot on the backdrop of Camelback Mountain, Kate Brosnahan (Spade) in the green sweater, Mike Carter in the back row center, next to Andy Spade and me on the end.

Choices That Shaped My Future

My entrepreneurial path in college was not limited to retail; it also included other ventures. I joined Beta Alpha Psi, the honorary accounting society, which required a strong GPA. The real value, if we are honest, was the cocktail receptions with the

Big 8 firms. Networking, in my humble opinion, is the most important course. It also comes with free drinks and appetizers.

At one of the receptions, I met Chris from Coopers and Lybrand. I asked for an internship. He said they only took graduate students. I remembered my parents' lesson. If the door does not exist, build one. I persuaded him to give me a six-week trial. Self-advocacy opened the door and became a turning point. Success rarely lands on your doorstep. You have to knock very loudly sometimes. In the Tax Department, I worked under Bernie Kaufman, a gruff and brilliant individual. He taught me estate and trust tax prep, starting with calling family members to gather tax documents. Those calls turned into windows on family dynamics with side stories about siblings and paperwork drama. It was my first honest look at how business and personal lives intertwine, and it was a quick PhD in death and greed.

Meanwhile, my personal life was moving fast. My seven-year on-again, off-again relationship ended. I met a successful First Amendment lawyer, David Bodney, who was absolutely brilliant, extremely funny, and also from Kansas City. At twenty-two, I got swept off my feet, and I married right after graduation, a choice my mother opposed because of my age. I was sure I knew best. Youthful confidence can actually turn out to be wrong in hindsight. My mother was right about this one.

As graduation neared, I had two offers: Coopers and Lybrand, where I had interned, and Touche Ross. Touche Ross offered a better salary and felt like a better fit with the partners, so I said yes. That decision reinforced a few core instincts: advocate for yourself, seize opportunities, and build authentic relationships. People open doors. Results keep them open.

These experiences taught me that success hinges on your ability to communicate value and invite others to take a chance on you. It's about learning to sell the vision and then delivering on it. Those lessons carried me from corporate America into entrepreneurship and into motherhood.

In A Nutshell

My upbringing, experiences, and the people around me have become valuable assets in both business and at home.

So will yours.

My parents modeled hard work, service, and protecting family time, even when life was busy. My grandparents instilled in me perseverance and the habit of creating opportunities. Early jobs taught independence, problem-solving, and basic finance.

Childhood creativity and make-believe nurtured my entrepreneurial spirit. Structure at home shaped my approach to work-life balance. Accounting sharpened skills that later proved essential.

College taught me to trust my instincts, grab opportunities, and network with intention. Carter's showed me how culture and mentorship power a company.

Those skills translated into corporate life, where problems got bigger, stakes got higher, and the learning accelerated. Independence and proactive decision-making helped me navigate complex organizations and make significant decisions. The networking muscles I built in school turned into lasting professional relationships. The positive culture I loved at Carter's influenced how I built and led teams. In the next chapter, I'll show how those foundations evolved during my corporate career and how they set the stage for the leap into entrepreneurship, along with the never-boring project of balancing leadership and parenthood.

Reflection Questions

- Who were the key people in your early life? How did they shape your work ethic, values, or approach to challenges?
- Think back to your childhood. What experiences or activities nurtured your entrepreneurial spirit or problem-solving skills?
- Recall a time when you had to be independent or self-reliant at a young age. How did that shape your character or skills?
- What early indicators of your current interests or strengths can you see in childhood or school?
- Which early jobs taught you lessons that you still use today? What are they?

CHAPTER 2

Life in Corporate America

"If your actions inspire others to dream more, learn more, do more, and become more, you are a leader."
—John Quincy Adams

When most people think about transitioning from corporate life to entrepreneurship, they often envision leaving their corporate world behind completely. I thought the same thing. What I never expected was that my years in corporate America would actually become the foundation for building a business that supports working parents instead of burning them out.

Think about the skills required to raise a family: patience, flexibility, managing chaos, problem-solving, and being able to function on very little sleep. Now think about the skills required to run a business. Notice any overlap? I eventually did, too, but not right away.

It took thirteen years in corporate America for me to realize how closely those worlds relate. If you are worried about balancing business growth with family or about building a culture that supports parents rather than punishing them, I get it. What surprised me was that so many of the answers came from my corporate experience rather than from outside it.

Just as the lessons from my childhood, the lessons from corporate life did not appear gently or quickly. They came through hard work, challenges, victories, and personal loss. But together, they formed something I didn't see coming: a belief that family life and professional success can coexist without competing with each other.

Those corporate years taught me things like:

- Success comes from competence and respect, not age or job title.
- Opportunities often show up disguised as problems.
- Someone with a fresh perspective can see what experts miss.
- Technical skills matter, but emotional intelligence matters more.
- Your first career may not be your forever career, but nothing is wasted. Sometimes there is no perfect answer, only the best choice you can make at the time.
- Hard work and joy can absolutely coexist.
- The right culture turns long hours into something that feels meaningful.
- Real success isn't just about financial results; it also includes positive impact.
- Leading a team and raising a family both require patience, flexibility, and calm under pressure.

- Balance is not about separation; it is about integration.
- A supportive environment benefits both business and family.

People often describe corporate life as climbing a ladder, but for me, it felt more like I continued to build the ladders to climb. Still, it taught me what works, what doesn't, and what I wanted to do differently.

Let me take you back to 1987, where this chapter of my life begins.

Early Career

I have no regrets about getting my accounting degree. It was like working on a jigsaw puzzle, except the pieces were debits and credits, and the reward was a balanced set of books, rather than a picture of a waterfall. I loved putting all the pieces together and seeing everything fall into place. Assets equal liabilities plus owner's equity; balancing made sense to me. It was math with clear answers and no room for subjective opinions. My brain has always loved certainty and numbers. And honestly, accounting is a great foundation for anyone who wants to run a company one day.

But if I'm being frank, I got bored with public accounting pretty quickly.

I remember sharing an office with my manager at Touche Ross in 1987. She had been there seven years and was still doing the same work I had just started. I enjoyed organizing and cross-referencing workpapers, but I also thought to myself, I cannot still be doing this in seven years. So, after eighteen months, I decided to move on.

Initially, I considered attending law school. Instead, life intervened. A former tax client, Rudy Vucekovich, called me. Rudy was a serial entrepreneur who was an early executive at Yellow Front, one of the original discount retailers in Arizona. He asked if I could help him build a business plan and financial forecasts for a startup in the office products warehouse club space. Staples was just launching on the East Coast, so it felt like a big opportunity. The business was called The O.P. Club, a 20,000 square foot membership warehouse for office supplies. I spent hours building Lotus 123 spreadsheets and financial models with a consulting partner and finance wiz Irene D'Amico. With the plan and Rudy's track record, we successfully raised $6 million from three venture capital firms.

Right after the money came in, Rudy and the investors asked me to become the Controller. This came with a $29,000 salary increase, which more than doubled my previous salary. Law school disappeared from my future very quickly.

Within 18 months of graduating from college, I felt like I was on fire. I suddenly found myself managing the back office and accounting operations for Rudy's Phoenix-based chain of traditional office product stores. Rudy launched The O.P. Club by buying a chain of four stores called Ad King Office Products.

<u>My responsibilities included:</u>

- Choosing the technology platform and accounting software for The O.P. Club

- Managing an accounting team of clerks who had been at the company for over ten years
- Figuring out how to lead a team when I was 23 and most of them could have been my parents

They definitely don't teach you that in college. There were no textbooks titled "How to Manage People Twice Your Age While Pretending You Know What You're Doing." I was in way over my skis, but because I didn't know what I didn't know, I just kept going.

What I learned early is this: your first job doesn't have to be your forever job, but the skills you learn there can shape everything that comes next. And sometimes the best opportunities are just beyond what you feel qualified for, so you say yes and figure it out later.

Managing People in My Early Career

Of all the skills I developed in those early years, none proved more valuable or more exhausting than learning how to manage people. Looking back now, as both an entrepreneur and a mother, I can say with confidence: managing teams and raising kids require the same toolkit. Patience. Flexibility. Emotional intelligence. And the ability to smile while quietly wondering, "Is this really happening?"

One of my first big management challenges involved an employee with severe muscular dystrophy who relied on her boyfriend, the warehouse manager, for transportation. Sweet in theory. In practice, it meant that whenever he didn't show up for work, neither did she. Unfortunately, this boyfriend also had a drinking problem and serious anger issues. One day, he stormed into the office, lost his temper with the Chief Operating Officer, and was immediately fired. Just like that, she had no way to get to work. I remember feeling heartbroken for her and thinking the situation was completely out of my league. I was 23, managing complicated workplace dynamics that felt much bigger than me. That situation has stayed with me ever since.

Then there was an older woman in the accounting department who flat-out refused to have me as her manager. One day, she marched into my office, sat on my desk, and said to the founder, "You have to choose her or me." He looked at her and said, "Sounds like you've already made that decision." And just like that, she quit. I sat there thinking, was that leadership? Or did I just survive something?

I also wasn't great at delegating. Asking people to do things for me felt uncomfortable, so I usually just did the work myself. (A pattern that later showed up in both entrepreneurship and motherhood.)

What those early experiences taught me was this: leadership isn't about always having the right answer. Sometimes there is no perfect solution. There are only messy human situations that require compassion, practicality, and doing the best you can with what you have.

At the time, I felt overwhelmed. Years later, I realized those exact moments were teaching me how to build the kind of company culture I wanted, one that valued empathy, personal responsibility, and real human connection over titles and hierarchy.

Dedication and Growth in My Early Career

Managing people was only one part of the chaos. The real test came in the form of long nights, endless travel, and building stores from scratch on caffeine and adrenaline. I remember working until midnight, then driving for hours from Ontario to Venice Beach, California, rolling in around 2 a.m. just to start all over again the next morning, installing inventory systems, setting up point-of-sale software, and hoping the coffee was strong enough to function as sleep.

Within the first 18 months, we opened 9 warehouse clubs across Arizona, California, Utah, and Nevada. Rudy, the founder, would call me at all hours, very early mornings and very late at night. I became his unofficial "brain partner," translator, and fire extinguisher. My husband, David, at the time would joke that it was the O.D. Club (as in "overdose") and would say, "Now I get why his name is *Rude*-ee." As I mentioned earlier, he was very funny.

To put it plainly, I worked my ass off for two years.

I received a small stock option grant that eventually turned into about $15,000 when the company merged with Dallas-based Bizmart. That might sound nice, but compared to what went into earning it, let's just say it wasn't "retire on a beach" money, more like "put a down payment on a Honda Accord and keep going" money.

After a series of mergers, O.P. Club to Bizmart to OfficeMax, I was recruited by the same venture investors to join another company they'd backed. It was one of the largest IBM systems integrators at the time, transitioning companies from mainframes to AS/400s. The company was called Gateway Data Sciences, based in Phoenix with offices in Los Angeles and Irvine.

I started as Controller, but within weeks, I was convincing the founders to expand into retail technology. Somehow, they said yes.

Before long, I was:

- Getting us certified as a Value Added Reseller (VAR) for IBM point-of-sale hardware
- Convincing a software company in Poughkeepsie, New York, to let us be their West Coast partner
- Forming partnerships with Island Pacific and JDA Software
- Running the entire retail vertical for the company

These were exhausting but incredibly fun years. Retailers were finally moving off mainframes and embracing more modern technology. I was working insane hours, but I loved what we were building. The culture was electric. The founders worked hard, but they also knew how to have fun. It was the first time I experienced a team that believed success and joy could exist in the same room.

It was so inspiring that my brother even joined the company as a software engineer. We both still say those were some of the most fun years of our corporate lives.

And this was when it clicked for me: culture matters. You can push people to work hard, but if they feel seen, supported, and part of something exciting, they'll give you their best without burning out.

My brother and me at one of the infamous Gateway Data Sciences boondoggles
in Mexico to celebrate the success of the company.

Early Career Lessons

Those first few years taught me three lessons I didn't fully
appreciate at the time, but that would later become the
foundation for how I would lead companies, teams, and,
honestly, a household full of small children.

Lesson One: Leadership isn't about age; it's about competence
and respect. I was young, yes. I was managing people twice my
age. Sometimes they listened, sometimes they didn't, and
sometimes they sat on my desk and threatened to quit. But over
time, I learned: if you work hard, treat people with respect, and
actually know what you're doing (or at least try very hard to),
people will follow you. They may grumble, but they'll follow.

Lesson Two: Don't stay inside your job description; opportunity lives outside the lines. At Gateway, I could've stayed comfortably in the Controller box. Instead, I was pitching an entirely new retail technology division. I didn't wait for someone to hand me an opportunity to build one. That mindset of seeing it, going for it, and figuring it out later became essential in both entrepreneurship and motherhood. Neither comes with clear instructions.

Lesson Three: Culture is everything. Gateway showed me that high performance and high enjoyment can exist in the same company. You don't have to pick between a strict, joyless culture and chaos with beanbags. You can create an environment where people feel supported and challenged. That idea stuck with me and became central to how we built Serena & Lily years later.

While I was learning all this professionally, my personal life was teaching me some equally important and sometimes painful truths.

I had been dating the same person since high school. At 22, I got married despite my mother's strong intuition (which of course I ignored). My husband at that time was hoping to start a family, and the bottom line is that I was too young and inexperienced to be married. . . After three and a half years of marriage, we eventually divorced. And while I wouldn't wish a divorce on anyone, it gave me one of the most important lessons of my life: your personal life and professional life have to be aligned. You can't thrive in one and suffer in the other forever. Eventually, the imbalance catches up with you. What I learned in those years at work and at home is that life doesn't happen in silos. Everything impacts everything. You don't clock out of being a human when you clock into being a professional. And that belief would eventually shape how I built teams, companies, and a culture that made room for people to be their whole selves.

The Microsoft Moments

After moving to Los Angeles, managing Gateway's retail projects (and living on airport food), I began to sense that the company was struggling financially. When you're in accounting, you tend to notice when the numbers start looking … less than optimistic. So, I quietly began exploring other options.

I ended up reconnecting with Deloitte & Touche (formerly Touche Ross) and took a role managing their Western U.S. Retail Technology Consulting practice. I was back in a corporate environment, but now with experience in both retail and technology under my belt.

I was definitely living out my best single years in Los Angeles. I lived in a house in West Hollywood with 3 other very wild and crazy girlfriends. One story really stood out as a memory, and that is when I came home one night, and there were around 10 guys asleep on the floor of our living room. I said to my roommates, "What on earth is going on in the living room?" and Jill responded, "Aren't they cute? That's the United States rugby team." Those were some fun and crazy times.

Then a year later came the call that changed everything.

A headhunter called about a role at Microsoft. I couldn't understand why Microsoft would want someone like me. I wasn't an engineer, and I didn't have an Ivy League degree; at the time, Microsoft mostly hired those with them. But this headhunter was persistent. He kept faxing (yes, faxing) me articles about all the millionaires Microsoft had created. So, I said yes to the interview.

Here I am with my 3 wild and crazy roommates, from left to right: Myself, Jill, Eve, and Heather.

Microsoft was preparing to launch Windows 95 and sought to expand into the enterprise market with Windows NT and SQL Server. They were hiring industry specialists who understood large-scale business systems and could help transition legacy systems, such as the IBM 4680 and OS/2, onto Windows NT and SQL Servers. The retail industry was a big focus.

I still wasn't totally sure what the job entailed, but I had a gut feeling: this was a wave worth riding. After going through an extensive interview process, I was given the job offer at Microsoft in late 1994.

When I gave my notice at Deloitte & Touche, the Seattle partners called to talk me out of it. Since Deloitte was Microsoft's auditor, they told me Microsoft's growth had peaked after its first decade and insisted the stock wouldn't go any higher. I listened politely and then ignored them.

This was not an insider trading tip; these were partners trying to talk me out of leaving Deloitte & Touche.

I accepted the job as Head of Retail Vertical for the Western U.S. at Microsoft.

Career Highlights and Relationships

Microsoft was a wild ride in the best possible way. The growth was explosive. The company was printing cash. Assistants had stock options. Receptionists were buying houses. It felt like being at the center of a tech weather system that no one fully understood, but everyone knew was historic. One of the major projects I worked on was Microsoft's newly acquired e-commerce software, eShop. We needed a major retailer to adopt it and fast. Steve Ballmer (then President of Microsoft) happened to be a college roommate of Bob Fisher (Don Fisher's son, the founder of Gap). So naturally, I emailed Steve and asked, "Would he assist me with opening executive doors at the Gap and help me to pitch this?" And he responded within minutes, "Sure."

This was typical of Microsoft at the time. You could email an executive and they'd respond within fifteen minutes.

Steve called up Bob Fisher, who then introduced us to the CIO (Chief Information Officer) of the Gap. Thanks to that trust and connection, the Gap became our first major customer for Microsoft's Merchant Server.

And because nothing says team-building like mild chaos, the installation was a disaster. The software was still in Beta, and we were basically debugging it live. In tech, this is called having your customer "eat your dog food."

Note to self: involve friends in business carefully, especially when the software is still crashing.

Of all my experiences in the corporate world, I learned the most at that company. What stood out most was how deliberately they rewarded failure. It often seemed that the people who experienced the biggest mishaps were the ones who got promoted. The philosophy was clear: take real risks, be bold, and push the limits. That kind of behavior was encouraged and rewarded because the last thing they wanted was for people to take those hard-earned lessons to a competitor.

They routinely had multiple teams working on the exact same projects, creating intense internal competition that ultimately produced the strongest solutions. Thinking out of the box wasn't just encouraged, it was expected. In fact, if you weren't getting at least one flame email a day, you were probably not doing your job or challenging anyone enough.

Steve Ballmer left me with three especially memorable lessons. At a Global Summit with more than 7,000 people in the audience, he said: If you make a mistake, admit it. Don't try to cover it up. Say to the customer, "I made a mistake, and I'm going to make this right." He also told that same audience that if you didn't love your job at Microsoft and didn't jump out of bed every day ready to give 100% plus, you should leave and make room for someone who would.

I also got a huge kick out of how competitive Steve was. When Microsoft first launched Internet Explorer, Netscape held over 90% of the browser market. Steve promised that if we could get past 60% market share within a year, he would do a cartwheel on stage. Keep in mind, Steve is a very tall, stocky man. The image alone was hilarious and perfectly captured how evangelical and driven he was in rallying the company.

An Unlikely Award Night.

One of my favorite stories from my Microsoft years happened in early 1997.

Bill Gates had been invited to the Netguide Awards in Los Angeles to receive the Innovator of the Year award. Since I was the most senior Microsoft employee in Los Angeles at the time, the PR team asked if I could attend the black-tie event and accept the award on Bill's behalf.

For context, I had just started dating my now-husband, Marc Sarosi. This was maybe our fourth date. So naturally I said, "Want to get dressed up and accept an award for Bill Gates with me?" He said yes, probably before fully understanding what that meant.

We hired a black limo with a few other people to take us to the event in Hollywood. Halfway there, the car broke down. Full tuxedos and red-carpet invite, and we were standing on the side of the road in Los Angeles trying to hail a cab. Very glamorous.

On the way there (in the cab we finally found), my friends and I were brainstorming what I should say when accepting the award. That same day, the news had broken that scientists had successfully cloned a sheep named Dolly. So naturally, I got up on stage in front of a theater full of tech heads and said:

"Hi, my name is Bill Gates. We're beta-testing cloning at Microsoft, and as you can see, we're still working out a few bugs."

It actually got a big laugh.

The funniest part? The award is still sitting on the bookshelf in my library. I never figured out who I was supposed to mail it to, and nobody from Microsoft ever asked for it back. So technically, I still have Bill Gates' award. (Bill, if you're reading this, just say the word, and I'll FedEx it.)

This is Marc and me at the Netguide Awards in 1997, accepting Bill Gates' award.

A Culture of Success and Leadership Lessons

Microsoft in the mid-90s was unlike anything I'd ever experienced. The company was exploding. The business was wildly profitable. It felt like every single person, from executives to assistants, had stock options, and everyone was doing incredibly well. It was a front-row seat to one of the greatest technology growth stories in modern history.

I was also incredibly fortunate to have had a boss like Rich Kaplan. Rich was upbeat, approachable, funny, and believed in letting people create their own lanes. He gave me the freedom to shape my own role but always made time for regular check-ins. He was the kind of leader who made you want to work even harder, not because you were afraid of him, but because you respected him. Years later, he and I even recorded an episode together on the *Beyond the Blue Badge* podcast, which features former Microsoft employees sharing their stories post-Microsoft.

Microsoft wasn't just a company; it was a technology revolution. They built the operating system, and then thousands of other companies built their futures on top of it. Computer manufacturers, printer companies, and software developers were all designing for Windows. Bill Gates used to open many of his talks by saying, "I have great news to report: Moore's Law is still intact," meaning computer processing power doubled every two years while the cost was cut in half. He wasn't joking. You could feel that acceleration every single day. I like to say Microsoft put the gas on the right and the brake on the left.

Of course, like any place going through hypergrowth, Microsoft had some blind spots, too. I told executives more than once that if they wanted to win the enterprise market, they needed to own vertical application software. That was IBM's strategy. Oracle's strategy. The response I got? "We will never do that. We make platform operating systems and desktop applications, not enterprise applications." The level of confidence was ... impressive. (Spoiler: Microsoft eventually did build vertical enterprise applications.)

Sony Entertainment

One of my proudest moments at Microsoft came from an unexpected place: Sony Entertainment in Burbank.

Sony was building a wildly ambitious entertainment complex in San Francisco. Think: an urban Disneyland inside a five-story building, filled with immersive experiences based on children's books, restaurants, retail, and even an IMAX theater. It was futuristic, creative, and slightly chaotic, totally my kind of project.

Their Head of Retail, Harlan Bratcher, and I developed a strong friendship. One day, he casually said, "Why don't we build the first Microsoft Retail Experience Store inside the Sony Metreon?"

And without thinking too hard (as many great ideas begin), I said, "Why don't we?"

The idea made its way to the right people because this is another one of those only-at-Microsoft moments. I reported through Joe Vetter, who was a very close colleague of Bill Gates.

With Sony's help, I put together a full proposal, complete with renderings and a vision for how a Microsoft retail store could look and function. Joe took it straight to Bill Gates and Steve Ballmer.

And just like that, we got approval and an $8 million budget to build the first Microsoft Experience Store. Keep in mind that this is before Apple had its first retail store.

With one other employee at Microsoft, Michael Lapkin, and the partnership with Sony, we pulled off a magnificent and disruptive concept store in the heart of San Francisco. The store had so many cool gadgets and very cool technology throughout, even a self-playing piano running on Windows 95. We built a true lifestyle store using Microsoft software. This accomplishment awarded Michael and me the Frontier award at Microsoft, a new award that was created for people who were trailblazing and innovating, awarded by Bill Gates himself.

Here is the entrance to the MicrosoftSF Store at Metreon.

Here is Michael Lapkin and I receiving the Frontier Award: from left to right, Orlando Ayala, Jeff Raikes, Bill Gates, Myself, Michael Lapkin, and Steve Ballmer.

This project changed me. It taught me:

- Leadership isn't about having all the answers; it's about making space for new ideas and letting people run with them.
- Sometimes, not coming from a traditional background (such as engineering or an Ivy League school) can help you see possibilities that others don't.
- Networking isn't about collecting business cards; it's about building authentic relationships, so when an idea needs oxygen, you know exactly who to call.

What I didn't know then was that this project would be the beginning of a much bigger shift. In that business, social responsibility, personal purpose, and eventually motherhood would start to intersect.

Personal Challenges at Microsoft

Of course, it wasn't all innovation and standing ovations in theaters pretending to be Bill Gates. There were also some incredibly challenging and deeply personal moments during my time at Microsoft.

One of the first came from something that terrified me: public speaking. I had to speak at 3-4 conferences a week across the Western U.S. The first few times, I was terrified. I bought cassette tapes called things like "Conquering Your Fear of Public Speaking," and I listened obsessively. What I eventually learned was simple: if you know your material inside and out, the fear fades. To this day, if I'm speaking on a topic I know well, I'm totally comfortable. If I'm not prepared, I'm just like everyone else: hoping no one notices my hands shaking and my tongue sticking to my lips.

Over time, my role expanded to:

- Keynoting major retail conferences
- Speaking at CEO summits
- Meeting with executives from nearly every major retailer in the Western U.S.
- Partnering with countless software companies

One of my superpowers turned out to be networking. The Windows 95 era was exciting. Microsoft launched Internet Explorer to take on Netscape's 90%+ browser market share. We were describing a future that sounded like science fiction: streaming video, broadband internet, handheld computers, and smart homes. I'm not even sure we fully believed it yet, but we were saying it with confidence on stage.

But then life did what life does: it reminded me that none of this is guaranteed.

About 6-8 months after I joined Microsoft, I got the phone call that changed everything: my father had been killed in a car accident.

The strange part is, the night before, I had spent almost an hour on the phone with him, which was extremely unusual. My dad was not a phone talker. Normally, he would say a few sentences and hand the phone to my mom. But that night, 11/10/95, he spoke to me at length. He was heartbroken over the assassination of Yitzhak Rabin in Israel earlier in the week. My father deeply believed in peace between Israelis and Palestinians, and Rabin represented that hope. His grief was personal, and for some reason, he opened up to me about it that evening.

The next morning, he carried on with his day as usual. After finishing medical exams, he went to pick up my aunt for a theater show. While driving through Kansas City, he hit a patch of ice and was struck by a semi-truck. He died instantly. It was 11:11 a.m. on November 11, 1995.

That moment shifted everything for me.

Suddenly, questions that had been whispers became loud:

- What do I want my life to stand for?
- Is work enough?
- Am I ready for marriage and children?
- What is the point of success if life can change that quickly?

My father's death taught me that we have no control over how long we are here, only over what we do with the time we're given. It was the beginning of my shift from "success for success's sake" to "purpose and legacy."

It was also the moment I started thinking seriously about leaving corporate life, even though I didn't act on it for another five years.

Personal and Professional Growth at Microsoft

Amid the intensity of work and the grief of losing my father, life kept moving. In June of 1998, Marc and I got married, and by December, we moved to the Bay Area to oversee the opening of the Microsoft store at the Metreon. We packed up our lives, brought our three dogs, and landed in Mill Valley.

We knew it was home the moment we realized that every other car seemed to have a lab riding shotgun. Our "blended family" of three dogs fit right in. It was quirky, warm, and natural, the kind of place where you felt like you could build a life, not just a career.

That move taught me something I didn't fully appreciate until later: the environment you choose matters. Just like a business needs the right ecosystem to thrive, people do too. You can work hard anywhere, but when your surroundings align with your values and pace of life, everything flows more easily.

It was around this time that my Microsoft store idea, born from that "Why don't we?" conversation with Sony, was finally coming to life.

The Microsoft Store Experience

The Microsoft Store project officially took off in San Francisco at The Metreon, Sony's new entertainment and retail complex downtown. It was bold, ambitious, and slightly insane, so naturally, I loved it.

One of the requirements from the city during the build-out was that we hire team members from disadvantaged neighborhoods in the South of Market area. What started as compliance turned into one of the most impactful experiences of my career.

We hired an exceptional group of young adults, aged 18 to 25. Many of them didn't have college degrees, but they were brilliant with technology. They could troubleshoot PCs faster than I could log in. It made me wonder why they weren't working in serious tech jobs in Silicon Valley in lieu of retail jobs.

The answer was simple: not a lack of talent, just a lack of access. After exercising some of my Microsoft stock options, Marc and I established a small charitable family foundation. We funded 15 young adults through the Microsoft Certified Professional program, at $3,500 per student. I mentored them weekly. I watched them gain confidence, skills, and a future.

Time Magazine heard about the program while researching a feature on venture philanthropy, which involves people rolling up their sleeves and getting personally involved rather than just writing checks. They spent a whole day interviewing us and photographing the students.

Then nothing happened.

My mom would call every week asking if the article had come out yet. I told her I didn't think it ever would.

Then, about six months later, a Time editor called to verify names and ages. I asked if it was finally running. They said, "If Israel and Palestine don't reach a peace agreement at Camp David this weekend, we're running it."

I remember saying, "Well, if that's the alternative, I'm sort of guessing you will be running the piece."

Sure enough, on Sunday, July 23, 2000, the issue came out. Across the top are the words "The New Philanthropists." On the cover were six tiny headshots. You couldn't tell who anyone was, as I was trying to find the issue online the night before it hit the magazine stands.

I ran to the market the very next morning, bought a copy, and there I was, on the cover alongside Bill Gates, Steve Case, Paul Allen, Pierre Omidyar, and Martha Ingram.

And then a teenage boy in the checkout line turned to his dad and whispered, "Who is she?"

It was surreal. My mom, however, got a solid decade plus of bragging rights from it.

Not everyone in the program was a success. Three of the students landed great jobs at Cisco. Three were fired from the Microsoft Store for stealing computers. The others drifted out of touch when my life took another turn.

Here are the mentees in the technology scholarship program
I created at MicrosoftSF.

Here is the cover of Time Magazine when I was featured because
of the scholarship program I created.

Another project I'm incredibly proud of from the Microsoft
store was one that showcased how a corporate environment can
be leveraged for real social purpose. This was an event my
brilliant friend and co-creator, Alexandra Watkins, helped bring
to life: Tails of the City. The name was a playful nod to
Armistead Maupin's iconic San Francisco novels, and the
concept was just as creative.

We invited 100 artists to transform a simple Microsoft mouse
into a work of art, with the only guideline being that it had to fit

within a 12-by-12-inch box. The results were extraordinary. We turned the store into a stunning gallery and hosted an auction to benefit the Destination Foundation, a nonprofit granting dream trips to people dying of AIDS in the late 90's. We had mouse submissions from Kate Spade, Wavy Gravy, Bonnie Raitt, many artists in the Bay Area, and even a signed mouse from Bill Gates. It was mind-blowing how creative people were.

That night, we raised over $120,000 and had an unforgettable time doing it.

Here is one of the mouse art pieces submitted by Bonnie Raitt, Bonnie Tempesa, and Tom Rice, titled *Three Blind Gospel Mice*.

I became pregnant in the fall of 2000, after two miscarriages and being constantly on airplanes. It was finally time to leave Microsoft. I loved the work, but I couldn't keep traveling constantly while trying to start a family.

That was the end of my corporate chapter and the beginning of everything that came next.

In a Nutshell

Looking back, my corporate years weren't just about climbing a ladder. They were about gathering tools, skills, relationships, and instincts that I would later use to build a company and raise a family at the same time.

Every role taught me something I didn't know I would need.

At The O.P. Club, I learned how to manage people, even when they were older, louder, and more experienced than I was. At Gateway, I learned that culture matters, and that fun and hard work don't have to be mutually exclusive. At Microsoft, I learned how to scale ideas, lead without all the answers, build trust quickly, making mistakes is how you push boundaries, and find purpose inside a company that moved at the speed of light.

I learned some of the most memorable things of my career from Steve Ballmer, I also learned that business and life don't exist in separate boxes. Personal loss, ambition, burnout, and inspiration all walk into the office with you, whether you invite them or not.

The Microsoft Store project was the first time I saw how business success could drive social impact. It was also the first time I understood you could design a company to work for people, not the other way around. That idea stayed with me and became the foundation of how we built Serena & Lily.

So, while this chapter of my life ends with me leaving corporate America, it doesn't close any doors. Instead, it sets the stage for what's next.

In the next chapter, you'll see how all of this—every spreadsheet, mentorship, late-night flight, bad coffee, and unexpected opportunity—prepared me to build something entirely new. Serena & Lily didn't start with a business plan. It started with feeling a void in the market and having the chutzpah to go after it.

And it started with everything I learned from corporate life, just done my way.

CHAPTER 3

Love and Partnership: The Foundation of Success

"Behind every great woman is a man confident enough
to stand beside her, not in front of her."
—Unknown

As my phone buzzed at midnight with a pricing error on our website that went viral, I looked over at my sleeping husband, Marc, and felt that familiar wave of gratitude. I'd handle the crisis, and he'd be the one to wake up at 6 a.m. with our toddlers, make breakfast, and do school drop-offs (only mildly resentful).

Love is one of the greatest pleasures of the soul. But honestly, the word "love" is so broad it barely means anything anymore. I don't love my husband the same way I love my kids, and I don't love my kids the same way I love my dog or all my best friends. I always say I don't have a favorite child. I love each of them the most, but for totally different reasons.

But this particular kind of love, the partnership behind the scenes of every so-called "successful" entrepreneur, rarely gets mentioned in business books. It should. Because without that steady, unglamorous kind of partnership, a lot of dreams would never make it past a PowerPoint pitch deck.

Here's what I've learned about love and partnership (the real version, not the fairytale):

- Romantic love is cute, but actual love takes 20+ years and a shared life of ups and downs.
- Compatibility is part chemistry, part careful decision-making, part who owns what domains in the household.
- It takes a special kind of man not to be the primary breadwinner and not let it wreck his ego.
- Friction isn't a bad thing; it's how diamonds (and healthy relationships) get polished.
- Two type-A people in one house leads to high productivity … and occasionally kids being left on the steps at school.
- Men really are wired to be hunters, and sometimes they just aren't your girlfriend who likes to talk.
- The greatest partner test: Are you physically attracted to them, do your long-term goals align, and do you bring out the best in one another?
- Success without someone to share it with feels empty (and slightly boring).
- Many of us subconsciously choose someone who pushes us into our best selves, even when it's not pretty. I couldn't have built a multimillion-dollar brand with toddlers underfoot if Marc hadn't been home, quietly making it all possible.

This chapter is about that, about how Serena changed my professional life, and Marc made my personal life strong enough to handle it. I couldn't have built Serena & Lily while raising small children if Marc hadn't stepped in as the operational backbone of our home. Likewise, Serena and I are opposites in many ways, creating something neither of us could have built alone.

Entrepreneurship books love to talk about funding rounds and leadership philosophy. But rarely do they mention the 5 a.m. airport runs, the school forms that still need signing, or the partner who brings you coffee when you're running on no sleep and too much ambition. For women, especially, and for anyone balancing business with caregiving, partnership isn't a side note. It's infrastructure.

Beyond Fairy Tales: Real Love Takes Time

Romantic love, the Hollywood kind, is a myth. Real love, the kind that survives parenting, sleep deprivation, business failures, joint taxes, and Trader Joe's runs, takes decades. It is much less fireworks and more "Did you remember to transfer the preschool payment?"

My own love story didn't follow the traditional path. After divorcing at 25, I dated a lot. Not because I was lost, but more because I needed to get it out of my system. I was career-focused and happily independent. But around age 31, the math started kicking in:

If I meet the right guy now, we'll date for two years, get married for one or two, and then have kids ... and by then, I'll be 35.

This was before freezing your eggs was trendy, or even widely known. Biology was still very much in charge.

I didn't struggle to meet men (working in tech in the 90s meant being surrounded by them), but I wasn't interested in dating guys from my field. A male friend finally suggested I make a checklist of what I wanted in a partner so I could stop wasting time on second dates with charming disasters. Practical, right?

This was the 90s: no dating apps, no social media, no texting. You met someone through friends, at work, a matchmaker, or, in my case, through a newspaper personal ad.

Meeting Marc: Newspaper Ads and Destiny (The Pre-Hinge Era)

In January of 1997, I saw a personal ad in the LA Weekly newspaper that stopped me. It said he was looking for someone professional, down-to-earth, spiritual, fiscally responsible soulmate with integrity. And then: "I have so much a lot to offer, do you?" This wasn't the usual "long walks on the beach" kind of ad. It sounded grounded. Mature. Possibly emotionally available. A unicorn. I thought to myself, I check all those boxes, and yes, I do have a lot to offer!

To respond, you had to call a number, punch in a code, listen to his recorded voice message, and leave one of your own. Basically, the voicemail version of Tinder, but with worse audio quality.

His voice message made him sound thoughtful, sincere, and like someone who had actually done personal growth work. His outgoing message said something to the effect of, I've done a lot of work on myself, and I'm ready to meet the right person. I'm not interested in playing games. At this point, all I was meeting in LA were guys who were not interested in really settling down but rather just having a good time. I left a message that went something like: "You sound like my soulmate. I also love hiking, traveling, and dogs. I meet all your criteria except I'm 31 and about to turn 32, so slightly outside your age range. But I do have curves in all the right places."

I hung up and thought: wow, that was either charming or deeply embarrassing. Then I didn't hear anything for a month. I figured he was one of those shallow L.A. guys who only dated 22-year-olds.

But on February 6, 1997, he called.

Turns out he had posted the ad, felt ridiculous about it, and immediately flew to Africa for a month. By the time he got back, the ad had technically expired, but his voicemail box was still accessible. Lucky me. Or lucky him. Still up for debate.

The First Date: Chemistry and a Piano Bar

He asked me if I knew of any restaurants between Pasadena, where he lived, and Venice, where I lived, so I suggested a quaint and romantic place for dinner in West Hollywood called Orso, located on 3rd and Robertson. He showed up 45 minutes early because he didn't want to be late, then spent 30 minutes debating whether to flee because he'd met me through a newspaper ad. Thankfully, he stayed.

From the moment we sat down, there was so much chemistry, and we couldn't stop talking. After dinner, we walked across the street to the Four Seasons and had drinks at the piano bar until it closed at 2 a.m. There were celebrities everywhere; it was peak 90s L.A., and we were too busy talking to care.

We had such a great time. This could actually be real.

Here is the personal ad that Marc ran in the LA Weekly.

The Partnership Test: Real Life Isn't a Romantic Comedy

Our dates were not all champagne and sunsets. Marc found out it was my birthday the day after our first date, and when he came to pick me up, he walked into a minefield of flowers. There were six or seven bouquets, from my mom and from various male friends who I'm pretty sure felt sorry for me. He later told me he wondered what kind of situation he was getting into.

Then came Valentine's Day. He cooked dinner at his house, and I brought my beagle. The dog flew through the front door, leapt onto every piece of furniture like a furry tornado, and to really seal the deal, walked into Marc's closet and took a crap. Right there. First date at his home. Closet ownership established.

Most men would have bailed right then and there. But Marc stayed. Maybe he was intrigued. Maybe he was in shock. Either way, I took it as a good sign.

A spiritual leader we both admire, Rabbi Alexander Seinfeld, has a simple three-question litmus test:

1. Do you have chemistry?
2. Do you want the same kind of life, kids or no kids, faith, values, city or country, luxury or simplicity?
3. Do you bring out the best in each other?

Not "do you like the same music" or "do you both enjoy hiking." Those things don't get you through mortgage payments, sleepless nights, or closet-related dog trauma. These three questions actually do. Marc and I had yeses across the board. Chemistry? Yes. Life goals? Aligned. He even wanted kids. And most importantly, we made each other better, or at least more self-aware.

Friction Isn't a Problem: It's a Feature

I believe we choose partners who will force us to grow, not because life is cruel, but because growth doesn't usually happen on a beach with a sunset cocktail. As Rabbi Seinfeld has taught us through the years, friction polishes the diamond. It's uncomfortable. It's loud sometimes. But it makes you shine. It's all about introspection on what part I am contributing to this friction and polishing myself.

Marc and I both have strong personalities. I move very fast, make quick decisions, and come up with five new ideas before breakfast. Marc is methodical, calm, and steady. He could sit with a thought for hours. Together, we are balanced. Or chaotic. Depends on the day.

But that balance is exactly what became our secret advantage in our relationship, in parenting, and later in business.

Proposal, Africa, and Alignment

Eight months into dating, he proposed. We were hiking near Steep Ravine on Mt. Tam in Marin County during Rosh Hashanah in October of 1997. Neither of us knew it would be the exact area we'd eventually live in for decades and raise our children.

A little bit about Marc's professional life, he built a successful gemstone business in Africa, right after college he went to Zaire (now the Democratic Republic of the Congo or DRC) he was a geologist and was hired to prospect for Emeralds, he quickly learned how to mine gemstones and acquired the mining rights in Zambia to mine Aquamarine and spent five years building a successful gem business in Africa. He and I shared a love for travel, so Marc invited me on a month-long trip to Africa to show me his world.

Cape Town, Victoria Falls, Zambia, Namibia, Tanzania, Ngorongoro Crater, Serengeti, and Zanzibar. By the end of it, I didn't just love Africa, I loved the clarity it gave me. This was the man I could build a life with.

We married nine months after our engagement at the Hotel Bel-Air in June 1998. Paid for the wedding 50/50; no one was "the provider"; we were building something shared, and our honeymoon back in Africa, of course.

By December 23rd, 1998, we'd moved to Mill Valley. It was everything we wanted: a town where dogs ride shotgun in cars, kids run barefoot in the park and slide down rocks in the creek, and nobody cares what you drive (at least not back in 1998). That was the moment I knew this was our place, our rhythm, and the beginning of everything else.

Our engagement photo with our combined family of Malaya (Mo), Jenna, and Snoopy.

Our wedding photo on June 14th, 1998.

Marc's family at our wedding.

Complementary Strengths: Not Clones

One of the biggest myths about partnership is that you need to find someone "just like you." No, you don't. You need someone who sees the world differently but holds the same core values. Values are non-negotiable; methods can vary wildly.

Marc and I weren't the same; we were complementary.

- I was operational speed. He was operational calm.
- I was future, vision, next leap. He was logistics, implementation, and what's happening right now.
- I was the accelerator. He was, occasionally, the brakes.
- And together, we actually stayed on the road.

That dynamic became crucial once Serena & Lily began. Marc took over operations at the factory, working directly with our cut-and-sew team. He handled production schedules, materials, and the supply chain. Serena ran design and creative, and I ran everything else: finance, vision, inventory, channel strategy. It wasn't perfect, but it was a partnership in action.

And at home? When I was making 24-hour trips to New York to raise capital, Marc was the one waking up with our three toddlers at dawn, packing lunches, dropping them off at preschool, letting me sleep an extra hour. That's real love.

The Entrepreneur's Marriage Challenge

Here's the truth most business books politely skip over: it is very hard to build a thriving company, raise children, and stay happily married all at once. Something usually gives. For many of my incredibly successful girlfriends, marriage was the key. Not because they weren't loving, loyal, or committed, but because being a high-achieving woman can be ... well, a lot. Especially if your partner expected a different arrangement.

It takes a particular kind of man to support a woman whose career sometimes outpaces his, whose paycheck may be bigger, and whose calendar looks like an air traffic control screen. That doesn't make him "less of a man," but it does require confidence, security, and zero attachment to outdated definitions of masculinity.

Marc always had his own work and ambitions and was very successful, but his ego didn't depend on out-earning me or being the high-powered CEO. That made all the difference. Supporting me didn't diminish him; it strengthened us.

But let me be clear, none of this worked by accident. We were very clear about domains. I actually believe this is one of the most important things to figure out in a marriage. We constantly talked about roles and responsibilities. Who does what at home? Who travels and when? Who takes the call from school when someone gets sick and throws up? We didn't follow any traditional model, so we built our own system, one conversation at a time. And yes, we fought. A lot. However, we viewed conflict as an opportunity for growth, not a disaster. Our Rabbi told us, "Friction polishes the diamond." Translation: marriage is less about avoiding the rough edges and more about how you use them to shine brighter. Not "Am I winning this argument?" but "What is this argument showing me about myself?"

This also applies to business partnerships. Serena and I didn't agree on everything, not by a long shot. We had tense moments, passionate debates, and times we both thought the other had lost her mind. However, when we stayed grounded in a shared vision and mutual respect, our disagreements ultimately made the company better. Two brains, especially when they work differently, will always outthink one.

Finding Your Complement, Not Your Clone

Another mistake I see? Entrepreneurs and partners typically choose people who are like themselves. Same strengths, same temperament, same blind spots. It feels easy, but it's actually trouble disguised as harmony.

You don't need a mirror; you need a compliment.

Marc was steady, while I was fast. Serena was design and creative, while I was spreadsheets and logistics. They didn't always make things easier, but they made things better. If you both see the world the same way, you'll miss the same problems.

So instead of asking only "Do we love each other?" or "Do we get along?" also ask:

- Do they see things I don't?
- Do they challenge me?
- Do we share values, even if our methods differ?
- Do they make me better, not just happier?

A great partnership, in life or business, isn't two people moving in the same direction. It's two different people moving in one direction on purpose.

The Soul's Pleasure in Deep Connection

As our spiritual mentor taught us, true pleasure doesn't come from the things we consume, buy, or collect. It comes from the soul, from awe, from loving others, from creating something meaningful. Everything else, he would say, is just "counterfeit pleasures." Think fast fashion, too many margaritas, or a loud bar.

He used to explain it this way: you can love wine like a connoisseur, or you can guzzle it like a glutton. One honors the soul, the other numbs it, a good reminder in love, business, and pretty much everything.

I am in love with my people, my traditions, my community. I love learning, traveling, meeting new people, and finding little moments of awe in the world. I love my friends, my extended family, and, yes, our dog, who might be the kindest creature on the planet. Nothing brings me more joy than being together with my family under one roof.

And that's the point: success without someone to share it with is empty. My biggest sources of pride aren't companies or revenue targets. They're relationships, the real ones that require patience, forgiveness, and years of investment—the ones you can't buy, automate, or delegate. More than 27 years into marriage, I can say the romance never disappeared. It just deepened. It's no longer candlelight dinners and clever first-date conversations. It's building a life, solving real problems together, raising kids, forgiving each other, staying even when it would be easier not to.

It turns out the same thing happens in the best business partnerships. What starts with passion evolves into trust. You learn each other's language. You develop a shorthand. You don't just split tasks; you share ambition, risk, and vision.

Summing It Up

The right partner in love or business doesn't complete you. They expand you. They challenge you, support you, and hold the net while you leap off cliffs, building companies, raising babies, or both at the same time.

Having Marc gave me something no startup funding round ever could: stability at home. Someone who made breakfast, handled homework, and stood by me when things were messy and very stressful.

Having Serena gave me creative partnership. Someone who saw beauty where I saw spreadsheets and made sure our brand had a soul, not just a supply chain.

None of it worked because it was perfect. It worked because we chose the partnership again and again, especially when it was hard.

For entrepreneurs, especially women building businesses while raising families, your partner might be the most crucial business decision you ever make, and the one no one talks about on CNBC or in Harvard case studies.

As we move into the next chapter on building a family-friendly company culture, remember this: business and love are not separate worlds. How you build one influences how you build the other. The lessons we learn in relationships can make us better leaders, and the lessons we learn in business can make us better partners.

Success isn't just about what you build. It's about who you build it with.

Reflection Questions

- Which qualities in a partner, romantic or business, truly support your dreams?
- Are your current relationships pushing you to be your best self or draining you?
- Do your values align where it matters most?
- Do you see friction as a sign of failure or an opportunity to grow?
- What strengths do you bring into relationships, and what blind spots?

If love, business, and purpose are all connected, how can you start living like that now?

CHAPTER 4

Starting Serena & Lily

"Only do what you love. If you haven't found it yet, keep looking. Don't settle."
—Steve Jobs

L ife has a funny way of coming full circle.

"She gave up everything she worked for."

"What a waste of talent."

It stung, not because they were right, but because they echoed my own late-night doubts. But eventually I realized something important: success doesn't have a universal definition. Sometimes the greatest pivots come wrapped in small beginnings.

My transition from corporate executive to mother to small business owner taught me this:

- Your identity is not your job title. You can leave the business card behind and still build something meaningful.
- Skills transfer, even the weird ones. Spreadsheets and baby slings both turned out to be surprisingly useful.

- Motherhood sharpens business instincts: intuition, multitasking, timing, and patience.
- Community creates opportunity. Real conversations lead to real businesses.
- Perfect timing is a myth. You start when life throws the door open. Or kicks it open.

Before we get to the day everything changed, October 2, 2003, when Serena first walked into my store while I was in labor, let me back up to where this transformation actually began.

Finding Purpose in the Pause

I left Microsoft when I was pregnant with our first son. Calling it a "hiatus" feels generous; it was more of a pause, a deep breath, a moment between identities. I didn't know what was next, so I followed my curiosity.

I got involved in philanthropy. I was one of the founders and launched the San Francisco chapter of Social Venture Partners, modeled after the incredible organization founded by Paul Brainerd in Seattle and scaled by former Microsoft employee, Paul Shoemaker, now in more than 30 cities worldwide. All partners invested at least $5,000 each year, and we pooled the funds and made large grants of $100,000 to $250,000 to Bay Area nonprofits. Think giving circle, but we didn't just write checks. We rolled up our sleeves and assisted with websites, finances, strategy, governance, and many other unglamorous areas that actually move the needle. But something felt off. Spending donor dollars on a full-time Executive Director to oversee volunteers doing unpaid work didn't feel efficient. Being an accountant, I was trained to follow the numbers. In this case, the math didn't work.

The solution was simple: collaboration. We merged with the San Francisco Community Foundation, so donations could go further by sharing infrastructure. That was not a failure; it was a smart business decision applied to generosity. I've always felt that many nonprofits working in the same space should merge, roll up, and create economies of scale.

These early years taught me:

- Impact matters more than ownership.
- Joining forces can be smarter than building alone.
- Leaving corporate life didn't mean leaving behind everything I'd learned.

Sometimes the best path forward is not a straight line; it's often a zigzag.

Soul Searching and Social Impact

With SVP Bay running smoothly, my curiosity drew me into broader areas of work, including philanthropy, women's issues, global education, and my Jewish community. I met people who looked at impossible problems and said, "Well... let's start anyway."

One story stuck with me forever. Scott Neeson, working in Phnom Penh, rescued children from a garbage landfill and sent them to school. But he didn't stop with building schools; he also built homes, health clinics, vocational training facilities, safe houses, and child protection units, all on one condition: the kids must attend school. The problem was that parents kept pulling kids out to collect recyclables so the family could eat. Real life is complicated. Scott didn't walk away; he built solutions around humans, not theories. The Cambodian Children's Fund remains one of the most effective nonprofits I have ever witnessed, and it's an honor and a privilege to continue supporting the life-transforming work Scott's organization has provided for over 2,800 children. If you want to get involved with transforming the life of one person, I highly encourage you to sponsor a child at the Cambodian Children's Fund. It's the best $150 a month you will ever donate, and if you have more capacity, I encourage you to go visit your sponsored child and help Scott build this vision. It's the highest quality NGO I have ever witnessed. I can promise it will blow your mind.

That was the moment I fully understood: business skills can change lives if you're willing to rethink how you use them.

At the same time, my connection to Judaism deepened. Not in a religious sense, but more in a cultural and soulful way. Shabbat dinners, customs, traditions, and community made my life feel rooted and meaningful. This was all where soul pleasure resided. This perspective shift would shape how I later built Serena & Lily: business, purpose, family, and community, all woven together.

The Reality of Nonprofit Life

So, naturally, I dove in headfirst. I left Microsoft and accepted five board positions with nonprofits. It sounded noble. It looked impressive on a résumé. It was, in reality... a disaster.

Meetings dragged on for hours. Decisions took months. People debated the most meaningless items on the agenda while children needed food and shelter.

And then came fundraising. Let's just say I would rather give birth again than cold-call friends asking for donations. I hated it. I loved telling stories about amazing people doing magical things in the world. People would connect, get inspired, and give, which felt right, but turning friendships into transactions? No way.

What I learned:

- Knowing what you're bad at is a strength.
- Just because you can do something doesn't mean you should.
- My superpower was building things, not chasing donors.

Just then, life handed me a new assignment: motherhood.

Motherhood: A New Chapter

Our first son, Max, was born in 2001, about seven months after I left my corporate job. Timing is everything, they say. In my case, leaving Microsoft right before becoming a mother wasn't just good timing; it was life-changing timing.

Some babies fight sleep like tiny warriors, but Max came into the world like a Zen monk. He slept through the night, took scheduled naps, and adapted to just about anything. We'd take him to restaurants, where he'd happily take a bottle and fall asleep. No drama. No fuss. This kid made us look like parenting experts.

But here's the thing about type-A personalities: too much peace and quiet makes us itchy. When Max hit six months, I felt that familiar inner voice: *What's next?* During those naptime windows, I kept thinking about all the beautiful baby gifts we'd received, each personal, thoughtful, and so intentional. That's when it clicked.

What if there was a baby and kids store that felt just like that—personal, curated, soulful?

So, I did what any slightly restless new mom with entrepreneurial tendencies would do: I opened one.

Marc and I launched Mill Valley Baby & Kids soon after Max's first birthday. It was approximately 1,200 square feet of carefully curated gifts, personalized items, and four or five nursery collections styled to resemble real rooms. We didn't know it then, but those room vignettes would change everything. Expectant mothers would walk in, see a fully designed nursery, and basically whisper, "I'll take all of it."

Success came fast, faster than we expected. By November 2002, just a few months after opening, we had outgrown our space. We expanded to 3,300 square feet. The business tripled. Our store became the nursery destination in the Bay Area.

To outsiders, though, it looked like I had completely lost my mind. I could practically hear the whispers: "She left Microsoft... for a baby store?" It stung. My identity had been wrapped in corporate life, keynote stages, and my business card of being at one of the most exciting companies in the technology industry. Switching out of that world was emotionally harder than it seemed from the outside. But here's what no one saw: I was walking Max down to the store in a stroller, laying him gently in the display crib, and helping moms design nurseries while my baby napped. It wasn't a step backward. It was the first step toward building something that blended all parts of me: mother, entrepreneur, creator.

And of course, just when everything found its rhythm, life added a twist. Baby number two was on the way. And with him, a meeting that would change everything.

But that story needs its own moment...

Mill Valley Bay & Kids. I really loved our initial branding, which was just baby but then expanded to kids.

A Serendipitous Meeting

In October 2003, our second son, Ezekiel (Zeke), arrived, and with him came one of those moments you couldn't make up if you tried. On the very day I went into labor, an artist named Serena Fisher Dugan walked into our store, portfolio in hand, ready to meet the owner. Instead, she was greeted by our store manager, Lisa Sewell, who had to deliver what must still be one of the best lines in retail history: "Lily will love your work, but she's having a baby today."

The next morning says everything you need to know about me. Zeke was born at 2 p.m. on October 2nd, 2003. By 10 a.m. the next morning, I was packed and ready to leave the hospital. Most new mothers go straight home. Not me. We drove out to Point Reyes for pastries at Three Dog Bakery, then headed back to Mill Valley.

Here's where parenting logic met entrepreneurial logic: our two-year-old, Max, needed his 1 p.m. nap. So instead of heading home with a newborn during a period when a toddler needed a nap, we stopped by the store first. Naturally.

That's when Lisa handed me Serena's portfolio, a chocolate-brown envelope with pink polka-dot lining, filled with twelve beautifully designed postcards showcasing her work. It was thoughtful, elegant branding. It stopped me in my tracks.

Most people would've said: "I'll call her next week." I picked up my cell phone with a newborn in a baby sling and called her immediately.

"Weren't you the woman who just had a baby yesterday?" she asked.

"Yes. He's sleeping. When can we meet?"

Life balances things out. If Max was our calm, easy baby, Zeke arrived to make sure I stayed humble. I couldn't put him down for the first six months. When I called our pediatrician and said I thought he might have colic, he said, "That's not colic, that's just high maintenance." He was fine as long as we were holding him

So, there I was, every meeting with Serena included: me, a baby sling, and a baby who insisted on being worn like an accessory at all times. That newborn was in every brainstorm, every design conversation, every early plan for what would become Serena & Lily.

Messy? Yes. Inconvenient? Absolutely. The start of something big? Definitely.

The Beginning of Something Big

I'm wearing a baby sling with Zeke attached to me like an adorable but slightly demanding accessory, and Serena walks in carrying three portfolios that would change the course of my life. This was not a boardroom negotiation; this was a baby store meeting, with spit-up on the clothes and billion-dollar potential floating quietly in the air.

Serena opens her first portfolio—decorative painting projects. Instantly, I can picture them across an entire wall of the store.

"I love it," I say. "How about we paint this entire wall into four room vignettes? A girl's nursery, a boy's nursery, big boy room, big girl room. We'll do a 15 percent referral fee. You leave your cards. Deal?"

She doesn't hesitate. Deal number one: done.

Then she pulls out portfolio number two—children's artwork. I already have a wholesale kids' art business selling to seventy stores, but I need more, especially for girls' rooms.

So, I say, "Want to create a collection?"
Deal number two: done.

Then she pulls out portfolio number three—textiles. Hand-block printing. Custom patterns. Something shifts. These aren't just pretty designs. This is white space in the market waiting for a brand to exist.

I say it out loud: "There's a real void in the market for elevated crib bedding. Nothing exists for parents who want sophisticated, beautiful nurseries."

Serena doesn't pause. "I agree. If I were having a baby today, what I would want doesn't exist."

She knows the market well; she's been a freelancer for Pottery Barn Kids, painting bunnies, bears, and all the overly sweet nursery themes you can imagine. Everything is cute. Nothing is elevated. So, I asked, "Do you have a concept?"

She nodded. "I do."

"Okay. Bring it to me. Let's do a crib bedding line."

Three portfolios. Two hours. One baby who would not be put down. And three deals.

When she left the store, she called her husband at that time and said, "I think something big just happened."

She was right.

CHAPTER 5

Growing the Brand

"If you want to go fast, go alone.
If you want to go far, go together."
—African Proverb

Success in business often comes down to moments, the split-second decisions that alter your path forever. That October day in 2003, when Serena walked into my Mill Valley store, could have been just another customer interaction. Instead, it sparked a partnership that would transform both the design industry and our lives.

Most people would call it crazy to start a company with someone you just met while caring for a newborn, no less. But Serena and I didn't exactly ease our way in. She painted four children's rooms in the store, brought in artwork for girls' rooms, and, six weeks later, showed up with around 15 crib bedding designs. My first-ever migraine followed shortly after. Whether it was postpartum hormones, or my brain trying to catch up with Serena's wildly original ideas, I now see that headache as the first sign we were onto something big.

Looking back, my transition from running a small shop to co-founding a major brand taught me a few important truths:

- Intuition matters more than industry experience, especially when paired with determination.
- The right partner multiplies your strengths.
- Outsiders often see what insiders miss.
- Timing favors the prepared.
- Crises produce creative solutions.
- Customers can be your problem-solvers.
- The best team members value both excellence and integrity.
- Bold moves require equal parts faith and strategy.
- And life-changing moments usually show up disguised as ordinary days.

Traditional wisdom says you need market research, business plans, and endless strategy meetings to start a company. We had none of that. What we did have was a shared belief that parents deserved better design for their kids' rooms and enough courage (or naïveté) to make it happen.

That belief solidified during a trip to the Atlanta Gift Market, where we walked through aisle after aisle of the same tired offerings. There were brands like Gordonsbury, House, and Shabby Chic everywhere. It was confirmation: the industry was overdue for a shake-up.

This chapter is about how we went from that conversation to our first production run in under a year. It's a story about partnership, persistence, and ignoring the rulebook.

No Experience, Maximum Determination

I told Serena I'd put in $50,000 and we'd be equal partners. Fast forward two and a half years, and I'd invested $1 million. I structured it all as "due to the founder" instead of equity, so we'd always stay 50/50. Because honestly, without Serena, there would be no Serena & Lily. And without me, the same story.

Neither of us had ever developed products or worked in the textile manufacturing industry. I walked her around the store, showing her how crib sets were constructed and asking her to imagine how her design sensibility could reinvent them. She'd go home, redesign, and come back. Our combined "experience" at that point was Serena making hand-blocked pillows with a local seamstress. Any sane advisor probably would've told us to stop immediately and hire experts. Luckily, we weren't listening.

We approached everything one step at a time. Serena already knew how to create textile repeats. We networked our way to the Korean textile printers in Los Angeles. One introduction led us to William, a printing agent. Days later, we were on a plane to L.A.

The minimum order? 3,000 yards per design. We needed 10-15 yards. We could not afford the minimums, but instead we pitched the future: "We're going to be a multi-million-dollar account." Was it true? Only in our imaginations. But William, maybe intrigued or amused, finally said yes.

At that first meeting, I remembered my time studying in Asia for my Executive MBA, a very important learning experience. I made a point of taking the owner of the Korean print shop's business card with both hands, which is proper cultural etiquette. Then, minutes later, both Serena and I dropped our cards on the floor. We tried to gracefully pick them up without crawling under the table. Not our finest moment, but very on-brand for us then: respectful, determined, slightly chaotic, and a very good laugh later.

And that's how it began, two women with the crazy gene with no manufacturing experience, no business plan, one screaming baby, and an idea big enough to make us think we were Ralph Lauren out of the gates.

Building the Brand Identity

Our brand identity started in the most honest way possible, with my six-month-old son Zeke as our first baby model. His big brother Max joined in, and together they helped define the soul of Serena & Lily: joyful, natural, and just a little bit mischievous. Those early photos weren't glossy or overproduced; they were real. And that authenticity became our secret weapon. Our first lookbook broke every rule in the baby industry. Instead of product specs or fabric details, each collection told a story, usually through the personality of a child. The opening line read straight from the heart:

"In a world of the familiar, what's left that's new? Only birth, new life. We see it in our garden in the spring. We see it in moments of inspiration and true creativity. We see it in our newborn babies. It is this spirit that we have brought to our first Serena & Lily collection."

No one else was doing that. Baby brands were still selling pastels with bunnies in plastic bags. So we ditched the vinyl-zippered packaging and put everything in beautiful hat-like boxes with little see-through windows. The packaging was so gorgeous that store owners actually displayed it, not just stocked it.

At our first trade show, the ABC Kids Expo, those magnificent boxes helped us book more than 100 orders with 50% deposits. Not because we were the biggest brand, but because we looked like we knew what we were doing... even when we were figuring it out as we went.

People ask how Serena & Lily became a brand so quickly. My answer: Serena never designed for what would sell the most; she designed for what felt new and different. We believe great brands are built on creativity, not spreadsheets. This is where one of our favorite office jokes began: Our fabulously talented and hilarious merchant Kate Lesher taught us the acronym "KIM," which stood for "Known Identified Markdown." It was code for Serena's favorite design, the one with bold colors or a wild pattern that wouldn't sell in large quantities but would end up on the cover of our catalog and make people fall in love with the brand.

That's what set us apart. While others chased trends, we created a visual language that felt distinct yet timeless, which we later called "New Traditional." Classic, but not old. Playful, but not childish. Artistic, but still livable. People often used the word "fresh" to describe the brand.

We weren't building a trend. We were building a legacy.

And we did it before we ever produced a single crib set.

Market Entry: When Timing Meets Preparation

People love to attribute success to luck, but in reality, luck is just preparation meeting opportunity when you're fueled by caffeine and adrenaline. Our "lucky break" happened Memorial Day weekend 2004, and it couldn't have been scripted any better if Hollywood tried.

After months of work, we mailed our first catalog to 800 baby boutique stores nationwide. These were the kinds of stores that carried high-end crib bedding and, almost without exception, one dominant brand: Wendy Bellissimo. She was the name in the industry, especially after designing nurseries for Hollywood celebrities. If you were having a baby in the early 2000s and wanted your nursery to be high design, you bought Wendy.

And then over that same weekend, Wendy Bellissimo faxed (yes, faxed) a letter to all of her boutique accounts announcing she was pulling out of small independent stores to go mass-market with Babies "R" Us.

In other words, she left the building just as our catalog walked in.

The timing was beyond serendipitous. Six hundred independent stores had empty shelves, anxious customers, and no upscale crib bedding to offer them. Meanwhile, our fax machine was spitting out orders like it was malfunctioning. Within weeks, we had nearly 100 wholesale orders, each meeting our $1,000 minimum. That's roughly $100,000 in revenue.

One small detail: we had zero inventory. Not a single finished product. Just beautifully styled photos, sheer nerve, and some fabric strike-offs and cut-and-sew samples.

So yes, we won the lottery. We just hadn't built the factory yet.

From Samples to Scale: Creative Problem Solving

The high from $100,000 in orders wore off quickly when we remembered one crucial fact: we didn't actually have any product to ship, just pretty photos, prototypes, and a whole lot of confidence. To fulfill even the first round of orders, we needed at least $75,000 for fabric, printing, manufacturing, trims, packaging, basically everything except optimism, which we already had in surplus.

Banks weren't an option. Venture capital wasn't the right fit. And I refused to dilute equity, especially after already investing far more than my original $50,000. So, we did what moms and entrepreneurs do best: we took action. We got scrappy. Our assistant, Maureen Mulhern, picked up the phone and started calling every single store that had placed an order. Her message was honest, slightly dramatic, and incredibly effective:

"Due to an oversold situation, we're requiring a 50% deposit via credit card to guarantee you're part of our first production run."

In reality, the "oversold situation" was that we had sold everything we didn't yet have, but every store said yes. They were desperate for a new brand to replace Wendy Bellissimo, and our designs filled that void perfectly. Their deposits became our production capital.

Crisis averted... for five minutes.

My husband suggested that only a spouse who values marital peace could think that it was time to move Serena & Lily out of the back of the baby store. We had fabric bolts stacked next to strollers and invoices sitting on top of changing tables. It was chaos disguised as entrepreneurship.

So we rented a 1,000-square-foot office 3 minutes away. It wasn't glamorous, but it had room for desks, bolts of fabric, and most importantly, breathing space and a place to ship all our first orders.

Meanwhile, 600 crib sets were about to land on our doorstep with no one to pack, label, or ship them.

Which brings us to one of our best decisions: hiring heart over résumé.

Building the Team: Starting with Heart

The shipping crisis turned out to be solved, not by a fancy consultant or operations expert, but by Zeke's nanny.

Carina had the rare combination of laser-focused attention to detail and genuine care for people. One day, she was helping soothe my baby; the next, she was boxing crib sets with military precision. She became Employee #2 and stayed with us for over fifteen years. To this day, I say we hit the jackpot with her. If Serena & Lily were built on fabric and dreams, Carina was the stitching holding it all together.

Our first "official" hire was Serena's studio assistant, Maureen. She came over to help part-time, but her heart was in textile design, and eventually she left to become a designer in her own right. That early flexibility, letting people grow into roles rather than forcing them into boxes, became part of our culture.

Then came the creatives who helped define the brand's look and feel.

At our first photo shoot, from left to right: Myself, Maureen Mulhern (first employee), Serena Fisher Dugan, and Barb Ries, our fabulously talented stylist.

Courtney O'Connell, who had a full-time job elsewhere, designed our logo and catalog on the weekends. Serena's friend, Carter Hachman, helped us land on the perfect brand name, "Serena & Lily," which sounded like heritage even before we had a single SKU in production. And then there was Shahe Boyajian, the owner of our cut-and-sew factory. He took a chance on two women with no manufacturing experience and a wild amount of optimism. Over the years, he became more than a vendor; he became family. He understood our obsession with detail, quality, and meeting insane deadlines.

Even Serena's mom, Bonnie Fisher, jumped in, creating personality profiles for each of the bedding collections. She gave our crib sets actual characters—whimsical, thoughtful, adventurous—turning baby bedding into storytelling. That emotional layer became a key part of our brand's magic.

Within a year of Serena walking into my store, we were shipping to 100 independent stores nationwide. It was proof that our hypothesis was correct: design with heart, build relationships, and the rest can be figured out along the way.

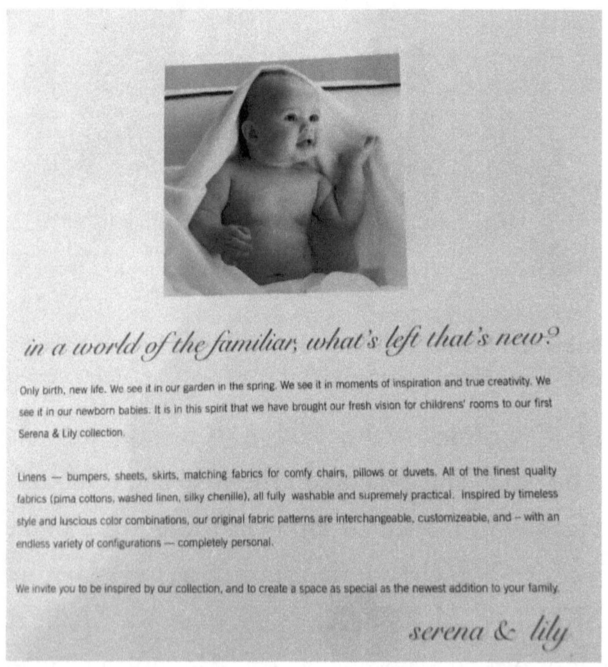

The opening spread of our first catalog, starring Zeke, the baby born the day Serena walked into Mill Valley Baby & Kids. He was six months old at our first photo shoot.

Our two-year-old Max also made his modeling debut at our first catalog shoot.

All our collections were named for children and had playful personality profiles.

In a Nutshell

People say the best partnerships are like marriages built on shared values, tested by chaos, and held together by mutual respect and a sense of humor. That first year of building Serena & Lily was precisely that. From meeting Serena with a newborn strapped to my chest to shipping our first production run, we learned more in twelve months than any MBA program could ever teach.

We learned that corporate rules don't apply to startups. While others were writing 50-page business plans and debating distribution strategies, we were sketching crib bedding on napkins, cold-calling textile printers, and telling factories, "Trust us, this is going to be big."

When banks said no, and investors weren't the right fit, our customers became our funding. When common sense said we needed industry experts, we went with our instincts and hired people with heart, grit, and a shared obsession with doing things well.

We also learned that building a business is a lot like raising a child. It takes sleepless nights, constant adaptation, a tolerance for mess, and a commitment to showing up every single day, even when you'd rather hide in a dark room (see: my first migraine).

Those early days taught us:

- The right partner changes everything.
- Resourcefulness can beat resources.
- Good timing is great, but perseverance matters more.
- Customers can be your biggest believers and your best investors.
- You don't need certainty to begin, just conviction.

As we head into the next chapter, where entrepreneurship meets motherhood in more ways than one, remember this:

- Some of the most life-changing decisions come disguised as ordinary days.
- Sometimes success looks like a baby in a sling, a partner with a paintbrush, and a fax machine spitting out orders faster than you can answer the phone.

And yes, sometimes the craziest ideas, like starting a company with someone you just met while recovering from childbirth, are the ones that change everything.

Reflection Questions

- What moments in your life seemed ordinary at the time but, looking back, changed everything?
- Have you ever followed your intuition over your logic, and did it lead somewhere good?
- When resources were limited, how did you get creative? What did that teach you about yourself?
- Who in your life multiplies your strengths rather than mirrors them? Are you treating that relationship like the gift it is?
- What risks are you hesitating to take because you're waiting for the perfect plan? What if the plan forms after the leap?
- Where can you trade perfection for progress? Or certainty for conviction?
- If your customers, community, or friends believed in you more than you believed in yourself, would you let them help?

CHAPTER 6

Building the Business One Challenge at a Time

"Starting a business is like jumping off a cliff and assembling a plane on the way down."
—Reid Hoffman (Co-Founder of LinkedIn)

If everything I've told you so far sounds easy, let me tell you it wasn't. There was plenty of stress and chaos, and there were days I thought, "Why didn't I just stay at Microsoft and get stock options like a sane person?" My husband loved to remind me that it was my easiest and most lucrative job.

One minute, you're standing at a trade show watching buyers swoon over beautifully packaged crib bedding. The next you're on the phone with a store in Beverly Hills, because three boxes arrived looking like they got run over by the delivery truck.

Starting a business is like building a house in a hurricane. Just as you're pouring the foundation, the winds kick up and start throwing debris—major packaging issues, cash flow, family dynamics, shipping disasters, and someone's feelings getting hurt because they weren't cc'd on an email. In the early days of Serena & Lily, every success came with a new problem, and every solution revealed a challenge we didn't see coming.

Those first years taught me some truths about building a business:

- Beautiful ideas still need practical execution.
- Family and business mix about as well as oil and water (or husbands and warehouses).
- Partnerships mean you share both the wins and the mess.
- Growth takes more than good design; it demands fortitude.
- Capital always comes with strings attached, even if you can't see them at first.
- Quick fixes usually create long-term problems.
- Vision is vital, but adaptability is survival.
- Trust your gut, especially with investors who believe they know everything.
- Some of the best opportunities arrive disguised as disasters.
- The hardest lessons are often the most valuable.

This chapter isn't about the glossy side of entrepreneurship. It's about the messy middle, the packaging failures, money scares, awkward husband dynamics, and the moments you wonder if you're completely out of your mind.

The Price of Learning

That perfect box seemed like such a brilliant idea at first—beautiful packaging that stopped people in their tracks at trade shows. Buyers loved it, placed orders immediately, and we thought we were geniuses.

Then reality showed up with a baseball bat. We shipped our first 100 orders, and no fewer than 70 arrived with crushed boxes. Corners smashed, windows popped out, ribbons mangled. It turns out that elegant packaging and shipping are not compatible life forms.

This was our first major go-to-market fumble, and it hit hard. It honestly felt fatal at first. But, like most entrepreneurial disasters, the solution was money, duct-tape thinking, and humility. We pivoted overnight, shipping the boxes flat, replacing the fancy packaging with vinyl, and redesigning everything for survival rather than beauty.

It was our first big lesson in business reality: a gorgeous idea doesn't mean a practical one. Some of our early choices were more "arts and crafts fair" than "commercially viable company."

And just when we thought we could move on, we were reminded of this mistake for an entire year. Serena and I would fly into a city, drop by a store carrying Serena & Lily, and like clockwork, yikes, there it was. One or two dented boxes on the sales floor, with the window plastic hanging off like it had been ripped open by a dog. I'd call Serena with my usual dramatic updates: "Emergency in Beverly Hills," "Window blowout in Pasadena," or "Box disaster in New York."

Painful? Yes. Educational? Absolutely.

Growing Pains and Family Ties

For the first two years, we did what most entrepreneurs do: we just kept putting one foot in front of the other. We built relationships with over 600 independent specialty stores, and it took everything we had.

Our team was incredibly lean. We hired two amazing young women right out of college, Mary Crofton and Shannon Flood. Carina Santos managed shipping and would bring in her sister when things got intense. And when that still wasn't enough hands, the husbands stepped in.

My husband, Marc, managed production at our cut-and-sew facility. Serena's husband at that time, Mike Dugan, ran warehouse and fulfillment operations. It was all-hands-on-deck, all-family-all-the-time, which sounds sweet until you're in the middle of it and realize you are now managing inventory, payroll, and marriage counseling simultaneously.

Without getting too detailed, let's just say that family and business mix about as well as oil and water, or husbands and warehouses. At some point, I actually wrote Serena a letter that said, in essence: "Either the husbands go, or someone's getting divorced, and I'm not just talking about Serena & Lily." It wasn't personal. It was survival. When production delays, cash flow, and baby nap schedules collide with marriage dynamics, things get ugly fast.

That was one of our first big lessons: starting a company is hard. Starting a company with spouses involved is... next level.

Evolution and Expansion

It was mid 2005, and Serena & Lily was really beginning to take off, and now here comes baby number three, Nathaniel (Nate). We now have three little boys under the age of four, we are still running Mill Valley Baby & Kids, and we have a rocket ship start-up beginning to blast off. Something has to give; we made a decision to sell Mill Valley Baby & Kids, and we completed that transaction by the end of 2005. One thing off my to-do list, phew.

We sold the store to one of our fabulous customers, Stacy and Lionel Achuck. If my memory serves me correctly, Stacy came in to buy bunk beds for her sons and also bought the store. Stacy and Lionel did an amazing job taking over and expanding Mill Valley Baby & Kids to three other cities. They eventually sold it, and ultimately it became Sprout and still remains as a baby and kids store in downtown Mill Valley in the exact same location we moved to in November of 2002.

As we grew, so did our customers' babies. By early 2006, parents were telling us, "We love the nursery... but now my baby is climbing out of the crib. What should I do next? Please don't make me go back to princess bedding."

Their kids had outgrown crib sets but didn't want to outgrow the aesthetic. So, like everything else we did back then, we said yes and figured it out later.

Serena designed and launched 10-12 kids' room bedding collections. Not just bedding—that would be too sane. We rolled out paint colors, lamps, rugs, and even some furniture pieces to complete the rooms. It was beautiful. It was also a logistical nightmare.

This wasn't just a product extension. It was an expansion in every direction: inventory, SKUs, warehouses, spreadsheets, working capital, and stress levels.

But it also taught us something important: Growth doesn't always show up with a well-planned business plan. Sometimes it arrives as a toddler climbing out of a crib saying, "Now what?"

The Capital Dance Begins

By mid-to-late 2006, it became clear that passion, duct tape, and caffeine were no longer enough to sustain Serena & Lily's growth. I told Serena, "We need outside capital." Our sales had increased from $750,000 in year one to $1.5 million in year two and were on track to exceed $3.2 million in year three, all while selling wholesale to independent retailers. Growth was exciting, but inventory and payroll don't accept excitement as payment. We needed cash.

Our original plan was to raise $1.5 million in a friends-and-family round. Nothing fancy. No Wall Street theatrics. Just people who believed in us. To get some guidance on valuation, I asked a friend for help. She introduced us to the CFO of a private equity firm that owned a luxury bedding company. Perfect, I thought. This is someone who speaks fluent duvet profit margins.

Serena and I went to their San Francisco office to meet him. Fifteen minutes into the conversation, he stood up, said he wanted someone else to join, and disappeared.

Enter: The Partner. He walked in like he owned the building, which, to be fair, he probably did. Without so much as a hello, he patted us both on the tops of our heads. Yes, like golden retrievers, then said, "You girls sure have been busy."

I wish I were making this up.

Then, as if he hadn't just reduced us to young children, he launched into how amazing our brand was and how beautiful the work looked, in a tone very much like a TED Talk meets paternal condescension.

We explained that we were raising $1.5 million from friends and family and were there to get some feedback on valuation.

Without blinking, he said, "My partners and I will take the whole round—one check. You won't have to worry about fundraising. You just focus on growing the business."

No negotiation. No due diligence. No hesitation. Just bad-a-boom-bad-a-bang.

Serena and I got in the elevator afterward, eyes wide like a billionaire uncle had just adopted us. Then the paranoia kicked in: what if the elevator was bugged? So, we stood in silence, clutching our handbags as if they were state secrets.

It felt like a dream. The kind where something amazing happens, but you wake up missing a kidney.

And yes, turns out this was too good to be true.

When Too Good Becomes Too Bad

A few days later, the term sheet arrived, and reality slapped us across the face with a cold, legal document.

There was a catch. Actually... several. The offer wasn't coming from their actual fund (you know, the one with rules, governance, fiduciary responsibility, all that official stuff). Instead, they were pooling money from their personal accounts—their partners, friends, and probably their golf buddies—to invest through a side vehicle. Translation: less oversight for them, less protection for us.

Still, it felt exciting. Someone wanted to write a single check for the entire round. No more fundraising. No more spreadsheets of potential investors. Just done and done.

I called an attorney I had met back in my Mill Valley Baby & Kids days, Cara Lowe. She specialized in representing founders and knew all the ways deals could go sideways. I sent her the term sheet.

Ten minutes later, my phone rang.

Her voice was calm but very direct, like the tone a surgeon uses before saying, "We need to operate."

She said, "Absolutely not. I forbid you from signing this. This is a terrible deal." For a split second, I thought: Is she being overly dramatic? Did we just hire an overly cautious lawyer? Should we get a second opinion?

But I didn't hang up. I listened.

She explained:

- The valuation was fine, but the terms were toxic.
- They wanted control, not support.
- If we ever disagreed on strategy, they could overrule us.
- They wanted investor rights commensurate with owning most of the company, even though they didn't.
- And worst of all, it came from individuals, not a structured fund, meaning if something went wrong, there was no official entity to keep them in check.

It was dressed up like help. But it was actually a takeover in slow motion.

And then came December.

The partner who had patted our heads (yes, that one) took over negotiations. He called from his son's soccer game, irritated before the conversation even began. He wanted to know:

"What are your salaries going to be?"

I said $150,000 each, the bare minimum we'd need to replace ourselves if we stepped out of the business. Mind you, I made more than that at Microsoft, and Serena was making six figures as an artist before we started this whole thing. And we'd been paying ourselves $36,000 a year for nearly three years at this point.

He lost it.

He said he wasn't discussing it until after the holidays. He knew our bank account was nearly empty. He knew the year-end was days away. He knew we were desperate.

And that's when my husband stepped in, calmly and clearly:

"No one talks to my wife like that."

We immediately secured an approval for a second mortgage on our house to serve as bridge financing. And while most people were wrapping gifts and drinking eggnog, Serena and I started dialing everyone we knew.

The 17-day fundraising sprint that followed would become one of the most stressful and defining moments of our careers.

The 17-Day Miracle

It was a few days before Christmas, when most people were baking cookies or arguing over who burned the latkes, and Serena and I were instead deciding whether to mortgage our homes or let our company die before its third birthday.

Rather than take the bad deal, we chose the more challenging path: raising $1.5 million from people we actually trusted—our friends, family, and a few brave souls who believed in us more than we believed in ourselves on some days.

We had 17 days. Our husbands thought we were crazy. Maybe we were. We made lists, spreadsheets, color-coded charts, the whole works. Then we started calling.

Here's what happened:

- 37 people said yes.
- Some wrote checks for $25,000, while others wrote checks for $300,000. No pitch decks, no fancy financial waterfall charts, just two very determined women saying, "We're building something really special. Will you join us on this journey?"
- We raised $1.5 million in 17 days. No fund managers. No term sheets with handcuffs. Just people who believed in us and trusted we wouldn't let them down.

I will never forget the love and trust shown to us by some of our biggest supporters. A dear friend I consider family, Norman Traeger, pulled me aside during a book event at his home and gently said, "I heard you got yourself into a little trouble. How can I help?" Moments like that stay with you forever. God bless these incredible friends and family, without them, Serena & Lily simply would not exist.

And then came the hangover.

Because raising money from strangers is one thing. Raising it from people you have to sit across from at dinner parties or see at school pickup? That's another level of pressure entirely.

I don't think entrepreneurs talk about that part enough, the weight you carry when it's not just about meeting sales goals, but about protecting the retirement accounts, inheritance plans, or rainy-day funds of people who love you.

From that moment on, every decision we made had a silent refrain:

Don't lose their money. Don't lose their trust.

If I had to chart my stress in those days, it would look like this:

- 10% operations
- 10% human resources
- 80% capital raising and cash flow panic

By 2010, the company had grown from $750,000 in revenue to $20 million, but each step of growth needed more inventory, more hires, and more capital. Exhausting doesn't even begin to describe it.

Looking back, was it wise? Financially risky? Emotionally draining?

Yes. Yes. And absolutely yes.

But it was also the moment we chose ownership over easy money, vision over ego-pats from private equity guys. And it set the tone for how we should have built the company from then on; however, sometimes your fundraising path is not as simple or discretionary as one would like.

Summing It Up

Every crushed box, every awkward investor meeting, every 2 a.m. panic over payroll shaped both me and the company. Those weren't failures. They were tuition payments to the real-life MBA of entrepreneurship.

The perfect packaging that arrived smashed?

A reminder that beauty without practicality is just expensive cardboard.

The investor who patted us on the head and called us "girls"? Proof that just because someone has the checkbook doesn't mean they should have the steering wheel.

And raising $1.5 million from 37 friends and family in 17 days? Equal parts miracle, emotional hostage situation, and masterclass in trust.

While my children were growing up alongside the business, I realized something important: success is not about flawless execution. It is about keeping your values intact while everything around you feels like it's on fire. My son Zeke taught me patience when he wouldn't let me put him down for the first six months of his life; the business taught me the same thing in a slightly different baby sling.

These early challenges weren't the end of the story; they were the warm-up. The real test was still to come: what happens when your company grows beyond kitchen-table financing and into the world of serious capital, serious stakes, and serious opinions.

The next chapter is where things get even more complicated: how to stay true to your vision when the money comes with strings. Because sometimes the biggest threat to your business isn't failure—it's success in the wrong direction.

Reflection Questions

- When have you learned something the hard way, and was it actually the most valuable lesson in disguise?
- Where in your life or business are you prioritizing "pretty" over "practical"?
- Have you ever mixed family and work? How did that go, and would you do it again?
- What relationships (personal or professional) need better boundaries to survive success?
- If someone offered you money for your dream but wanted control over it, would you take it?
- When has a setback secretly been an opportunity in costume?
- What are your non-negotiables when it comes to investors, partners, or growth?
- How do you balance keeping your business alive with keeping your integrity intact?
- Who are the 37 people you could call in your own "17-day miracle"? And do they know it?

Are you building something that can survive a few dents, or does one crushed box send everything into crisis?

CHAPTER 7

Building a Company with Unaligned Capital

"If I had to make a pie chart of my stress during those years, at least 80% of it would be capital raising."
—Me (unfortunately, not joking)

I spent so much time in spreadsheets, investor meetings, and capital raises that I forgot to enjoy our wins. Serena and I literally had to remind each other to stop, breathe, maybe have a glass of wine, and acknowledge what we had built. The day-to-day was relentless and could drain every ounce of energy and joy if you let it.

What those capital-raising years taught me:

- Timing is everything, like when our catalog dropped the same weekend Wendy Bellissimo left the boutique market.
- Hollywood moms can move a brand faster than a business plan.
- Every round of funding adds complexity (and someone new with opinions).

- The partnership matters more than the term sheet.
- Venture money often comes with invisible strings and sometimes handcuffs.
- A product-based business equals inventory, and inventory equals endless capital needs.
- Board dynamics can make or break not just your company but your sanity as well.
- Some battles are worth walking away from, even if millions are on the table.
- Success often shows up in the midst of chaos.
- Your belief in your vision must be louder than everyone else's doubts.

Between 2007 and 2013, we rode the crazy roller coaster of growth and financial anxiety. Jennifer Garner featured her Serena & Lily nursery in *People Magazine*. Bloomingdale's launched us in 17 stores. Our catalog business doubled. And behind all of that? A constant, low-level panic about running out of cash.

This chapter is the honest version of what it's like to grow a brand when your investors don't fully share your values or vision, when "yes" to money could also mean "no" to control. And how sometimes the smartest business move is walking away, even if your bank account disagrees.

Building the Brand Through Star Power

One thing we learned quickly: momentum is oxygen. One good thing leads to another, but only if you're paying attention. And in our case, we were so deep in production issues, packaging dramas, and shipping disasters that we barely had time to realize we were becoming *a thing*.

Then came Jennifer Garner. Designing a nursery for a Hollywood actress was surreal enough. But she didn't stop at being a happy customer. She asked what she could do to help *us*. Who does that? Apparently, Jennifer Garner.

The article, titled "Nursery Cool," sprawled across four glossy pages in *People* magazine and reached millions. The phone didn't just ring; it exploded.

Suddenly, we were designing nurseries and baby slings for Reese Witherspoon, Jessica Alba, Camila Alves, Britney Spears—and yes, each one came with its own mix of magic and mild panic. These weren't just clients; they were megaphones.

And that was our first real taste of what star power could do for a brand.

The Dance with Big Capital

By fall 2008, we were in our stride. We'd just launched our first Serena & Lily catalog to 85,000 homes, a considerable leap from wholesale into direct-to-consumer. It was expensive, terrifying, and precisely the right move. The response was strong. We could feel the momentum building.

Naturally, that's when big capital started circling.

A well-known Boston consumer venture firm reached out. They loved the brand, the growth, and the numbers. We were doing about $3.2 million in annualized sales, and they offered a $7 million investment at a \$12.5 million pre-money valuation. For a small, design-focused brand run by two women with babies on their hips? That was considered a premium.

And then came the closing dinner at One Market in San Francisco, where it all started to unravel.

The partner flew out to finalize the deal. Over drinks, he "joked" that he could always tell if a woman was pregnant by whether she drank wine. Serena was quietly six weeks pregnant and hadn't told anyone yet. She fessed up the next day, and he pulled her into a private conference room and grilled her about her pregnancy like it was a breach of contract. His last company had "lost a key employee to maternity leave," and apparently, he had trauma. We gently explained that founders don't take maternity leave the same way employees do, just as having a second child doesn't mean you abandon the first.

Still, that moment told us everything we needed to know about how this partnership would go. To sweeten the deal, he said he wanted legendary retail king Marvin Traub, the longtime CEO of Bloomingdale's, to serve as our independent board member. Not a bad idea in theory. So, we flew to New York to meet him the Monday after Thanksgiving.

I figured, we're already in New York; why not shoot for the moon? I overnighted our catalog and Nursery Design book to Marvin's office and asked if he or his assistant could help connect us to the head of the Home Department at Bloomingdale's.

Her response: "Mr. Traub does not make introductions for people he hasn't met."

Fair enough. Rejected politely.

But the universe provided a Plan B.

We called our secret weapon, Ken Rood, former President of Ralph Lauren Home and unofficial Serena & Lily guardian angel. Ken loved us. One phone call from him, and we were suddenly on Bloomingdale's calendar.

So, there we were, sitting at the Four Seasons Restaurant in New York (the power lunch spot, not the hotel), surrounded by retail legends. Marvin was holding court like royalty. And our VC partner? He arrived nearly an hour late.

Then Marvin asked us our first question: "So... which one of you girls has ever run a $50 million company?"

I just smiled. "We'll hire adult supervision when we need them."

But the real bomb came when Marvin asked the VC, "So, where does the deal stand?"

And he said: "Oh, we're just taking a look right now."

Just looking.

After 60 days of due diligence and a signed term sheet.

Serena later described it perfectly: "It's like being pregnant with someone's baby and they say, 'We're just hanging out.'"

That lunch and that sentence told us everything.

Marvin somehow still thought he was escorting us to Bloomingdales that day, and when he learned we already had the meeting set up with someone else, he exclaimed, "Fine, if you don't want me to come, I won't" as we collected our coats at the coat check, we both looked at one another and agreed, "Holy ego."

The deal was dead.

The masks were off.

But Bloomingdale's? We still got that.

Nursery Cool

Duo Serena Dugan and Lily Kanter outfit the cribs of Hollywood tots like Violet Affleck and Sean Preston Federline

Two months before her due date, Jennifer Garner admitted she had yet to nest. Whether she was busy chasing bad guys on *Alias* or just put off by the task of creating a room for a small person she hadn't yet met, she blurted out on Martha Stewart's talk show, "I haven't done anything at all!"

But inspiration struck soon after, as Garner browsed through a catalog from Serena & Lily, a nursery linens company that just two months earlier had sold $3,200 worth of crib accessories and fabrics to Britney Spears and Kevin Federline.

Impressed with the line's simplicity, Garner dispatched her interior designer to work with its creators, Serena Dugan and Lily Kanter. Their mission: "a space chic and comfortable and not overly babyish but still sweet," says Dugan, 32. The room, finished three weeks before Violet, Garner's daughter with Ben Affleck, was born, was earth-toned, soft and neutral. "They made the nursery feel comfortable, warm and welcoming," says a relieved Garner. "Serena & Lily's collections were classic and the cutest I had ever seen."

Garner isn't the only new mom praising the company, itself just in its infancy. Launched in May 2004, Serena & Lily quickly attracted high-end customers by eschewing clichéd themes like bunnies and duckies and bears, *oh my.* Instead they offered calm color

Launching a nursery linens line without the typical cutesy themes was a "leap of faith," says Dugan (with Kanter, right, at Kanter's home in Mill Valley, Calif.).

BRITNEY SPEARS After the singer purchased the "Henry" crib linens set (above) and 68 yards of matching fabric from an L.A. baby boutique in August, "we felt our company was really on the map," says Kanter.

Photographs by DEBRA McCLINTON

PEOPLE February 13, 2006 85

People Magazine spotlighting that we were the nursery designers for the Hollywood stars

Our shop in shop at the time of the Bloomingdale's launch at 59th and Lexington.

New Hope Emerges

After the Boston deal fell apart, it felt like déjà vu all over again, another near miss, another round of capital to chase. Serena and I were exhausted. Raising money feels like dating someone who orders the tasting menu and leaves right before the check arrives.

Then, out of nowhere, came a glimmer of hope.

An investment advisor called and said, "I just met these incredible women. Huge fans of Serena & Lily. They're starting a consumer-focused fund and want to meet you."

Women. Consumer fund. Fans of the brand.

Yes, please. Where do we sign?

We set the meeting for the first week of January. Of course, on that day, Northern California decided to stage a once-in-a-century rainstorm. The Golden Gate Bridge closed. Power went out across Mill Valley. Our office went completely dark.

Naturally, these women said, "We're on our way as soon as the bridge opens."

That was our first clue they were our people.

They arrived in raincoats and boots, dripping wet, sitting in our dim office surrounded by candles and battery-powered desk lamps. And within minutes, it felt less like a pitch meeting and more like reconnecting with old friends. They got the brand, not just the spreadsheets, but the soul of it.

By the end of the meeting, they said, "We want to invest. We want Serena & Lily to be the first company in our fund."

"Fantastic! What size is your fund?" I asked.

Silence. Then: "Well... technically... we don't have one yet."

A fundless fund.

Translation: "We don't actually have money yet, but we plan to raise it."

A dear friend, Lauren Levitan, had warned me: "Do not under any circumstances sign an exclusive deal with a fundless fund. You'll be stuck waiting while they raise money, and you can't talk to anyone else."

So, I took a breath and said, "We'd love to work with you. But we can only go exclusive if you invest $1 million right away."

To their credit, they didn't blink.

Two of the women, Kirsten Green and Rana DiOrio, each wired $500,000 of their own personal money. No committee. No waiting. No nonsense.

They believed in us enough to literally bet on us before they'd even raised their own fund.

And just like that, in the middle of a storm, in a dark office without power, we found new partners—the kind that knock down doors, or wait patiently for the Golden Gate Bridge to reopen. I'm also proud to report that Serena & Lily was the very first investment in Forerunner Ventures, a now $3 Billion dollar investment firm with seven funds, started by and led by our angel investor, Kirsten Green.

The Bridge Loan Breakthrough

Unfortunately, the fundless fund could not complete its initial round due to the global financial meltdown on an epic scale in 2008-09. Kirsten introduced us to another venture firm in Silicon Valley to complete that round. Eighteen months after securing that initial investment, life (as usual) delivered another plot twist: we were short $250,000 to make payroll and keep inventory moving because an investor failed to follow through on a verbal commitment to lead our next round.

Not a fun number to wake up to.

By pure coincidence, I was having lunch that day with a close friend, Scott Neeson, not your average friend, but someone who had left Hollywood, sold everything, and founded the Cambodian Children's Fund, an NGO at a Cambodian garbage landfill site. He was rescuing kids, building schools, creating homes; he was doing real, life-altering work.

So naturally, when he asked how I was doing, I said something like, "Oh, great! Except I had an institutional fund not come through on the verbal commitment they made to lead our next round of funding, and they will only fund a bridge loan if I can fill another $200,000, and we need it by next week, or my business might explode."

Without hesitation, he said, "I'll wire it today."

No paperwork. No questions about interest rates or collateral. He didn't even ask when he'd get it back.

Here was a man funding life-saving programs in one of the poorest parts of the world, and he still believed in me enough to front me the cash, no strings attached.

It was one of those moments that stops you in your tracks.

Because sometimes investors with millions will question your every move...

And sometimes the friend who lives on dirt floors in Cambodia will quietly send you $200,000 without blinking.

That bridge money kept us alive.

And it reminded me that capital isn't always about money. Sometimes it's about trust. Belief. Friendship.

And occasionally, divine timing and a lunch on the water in Sausalito at Le Garage.

The Great Battle for Control

Capital raising during these years was extremely difficult for a traditional consumer lifestyle brand, only very disruptive consumer ecommerce companies were raising capital. Even the venture fund Maveron, started by the founder of Starbucks, Howard Schultz, told us that even if Starbucks walked through their door, they would not fund them.

We were able to find a family office private equity firm that loved the brand, so we were funded again, but this time, the money came with a side of control issues sizable enough to fill a boardroom.

Almost immediately after closing the deal, the new investor sent in one of their operating partners to "professionalize the company." Translation: she showed up the night before our first board meeting, marched into our office, and demanded we redo the entire board deck, her way, before morning.

I was exhausted and needed to get home to my kids. So, I smiled and said something along the lines of, "This is the board deck. I'm going home to tuck my kids in. See you at 9 a.m."

This did not go over well. The next day, the tension around the board table was palpable. One of our long-time board members leaned over to me and whispered, "This doesn't feel like our company anymore."

And he was right.

That was the start of what would become a full-on ideological battle.

- Our Silicon Valley investors believed in "growth at all costs."
- The new investor wanted to hit the brakes and force profitability immediately.
- The operating partner delivered this message with the warmth of a parking ticket.

Now, the irony? She wasn't entirely wrong. Good companies do need to be profitable. But how you deliver the truth matters. And bulldozing founders, especially founders with young kids and no backup plans, is a terrible relationship strategy.

Less than a year later, the investor sued the company for "irreparable harm to his investment."

Irreparable harm. For a business that had grown 50% year-over-year.

We spent over $100,000 on legal fees just to respond to the complaint and sit through depositions. Money we didn't have. Time we didn't have. Emotional energy we really didn't have.

That's when I did something I never thought I'd have to do: I got on a plane, sat across from this investor, looked him in the eye, and said:

"This relationship is not working. You're draining the company. It's in everyone's best interest for you to be bought out, so we can settle the lawsuit and move on."

To my surprise, he said okay, as long as he got a 50% return on his money. (Quite a recovery in one year for an investment he claimed was "irreparably harmed.")

We were finally free... sort of.

Because the only way to buy him out was to take even more capital with even worse terms.

Which led us straight into the next chapter of this adventure.

Overpaying for Peace and the Deal That Would Haunt Us Forever

So, there we were, exhausted, sued by our own investor, and trying to buy back our freedom with money we didn't have. Not exactly the glamorous entrepreneurial story you read about in Forbes.

To make the buyout happen, our board chair and our original Silicon Valley investor came up with a plan:

- They would help buy out the problematic investor.
- They would then put in an additional $3 million to strengthen the company. In return, they wanted very aggressive terms, the kind you agree to when you have no options, no time, and no emotional bandwidth.

The price? A 60% return to buy out the investor who sued us.

And the new money came with a 2x participating preference, meaning: They'd get double their investment back first, plus their ownership percentage… before founders, employees, or early investors saw one penny.

I still remember sitting in that boardroom thinking: This is the kind of deal I'd give someone if I were robbing them politely.

When I protested, our board chair said, "We have no choice; if we don't do this, the lawsuit will bankrupt us."

And he was right. So, we signed.

Before the ink dried, I said something no one wanted to hear:

"We will never be able to raise another dollar for this company without giving the same terms to the next investor, and there is no way we will get out alive with that much preference on the capital stack."

Turns out I was right.

This was the cost of peace, not just in equity, but in leverage, control, and future optionality.

We had saved the company, but we'd also mortgaged its future flexibility.

Still, we were capitalized again, and we did what founders do best: we got back to work.

And in the middle of the 2008-2010 recession, when half our independent stores were going out of business, we did something no one expected.

We grew.

Which brings us to the next chapter of this roller coaster.

New Territory and Success Through Crisis

With capital back in the bank (even if it came at a painful price), we did the only thing we knew how to do: put our heads down and build.

In 2009-2011, we took two big swings:

- We expanded into adult furnishings and bedding, not just baby and kids.
- We sent our first full catalog to 85,000 households.

We didn't jump blindly. We talked to catalog circulation experts, ran the numbers, understood the risks, and still thought: Let's do it. And it worked. The response confirmed that our next big growth engine wasn't wholesale, it was direct-to-consumer.

And then something strange happened.

While the economy was collapsing in 2008-2009, we grew 50% year over year. Half of our 600 specialty retailers went out of business. Big home brands experienced a 30% drop in sales. Analysts predicted doom for any company labeled a "lifestyle company."

But babies don't check the Dow Jones before they're born. Homes still needed updating. And our customers, mostly affluent moms, didn't cut back on nursery dreams just because the markets were tanking.

So, while the giants downsized, we doubled.

We designed a room for the Traditional Home Designer Showhouse, and suddenly, socialites in the Hamptons were calling Serena & Lily their new favorite thing. We thought, "Why not test the New York market without committing to a Manhattan lease the size of a mortgage?"

We found a space in the Hamptons, formerly an antique shop, originally an auto body garage with roll-up doors. Charming, quirky, affordable.

Perfect.

But even with momentum and growth, we were stuck behind the scenes with a capitalization table that looked like a game of Monopoly gone wrong. Too many preferred shares. Too many liquidation preferences. Too many investors getting paid before the founders, employees, or early investors saw one penny.

At one point, we had multiple acquisition offers valued at $125 million, but with an earn-out.

Sounds great, until you do the math.

After investor preferences, there wouldn't be much left for the people who actually built the company and the early investors who made the company even possible in the first place.

That's when it hit me, you can build something beautiful and still structure it in a way that makes it nearly impossible to realize the value of what you created.

So, we did the only thing that made sense:

We stopped arguing in boardrooms.

We went back to work.

We opened the store in the Hamptons in the summer of 2013.

And just like we predicted, it was a huge success.

Serena & Lily's first store in the Hamptons in 2013. My family came out that summer, and 8-year-old Nate trained up as a cashier and had a blast training with the most fabulous employee, Kate Green. "Hey Kate, what's our sales read? Hilarious!" Some stories you never forget. Nate would ask customers if they were paying with a credit card or coins. I guess a term used in Minecraft.

The Real Cost of Capital

Looking back on our capital raising marathon from 2007 to 2013, I can say this with absolute certainty: raising money is not the finish line. It's the starting point of a whole new obstacle course.

Every round of funding came with a trade-off:

- More inventory meant more cash.
- More cash meant more investors.
- More investors meant more opinions, more pressure, more late-night board decks, and far less control.

We went from scrappy founders with a shared vision to a CEO and Chief Creative Officer navigating board politics, liquidation preferences, control provisions, and phrases like "2x participating preferred," which really means "they get paid first, and twice."

We learned:

- Celebrity nurseries don't solve cash flow.
- Investors don't always care about brand values or employees; they care about returns.
- Some partners want to invest in your vision. Others want to own it.

By 2010, the company had grown from $750,000 in revenue to $20 million, yet the stress never eased. Each growth year meant another round of funding just to keep inventory in production. I used to joke that I should've gotten a PhD in Working Capital Management.

The hardest part wasn't the work. It was the realization that, despite building something valuable, we had structured the business in a way that made it nearly impossible for the early investors, founders, and the team to win.

Some key truths finally sank in:

- Capital isn't free; it's the most expensive thing you'll ever take.
- The term sheet matters less than the character of the people behind it.
- A bad investor can cost you more than a bad year of sales.
- Control is everything. Lose that, and it doesn't matter how great your brand is.

So, we decided: stop chasing the perfect deal. Stop believing the next round of capital would fix things. Go back to what we were good at: creating beautiful products, building community, and betting on ourselves.

Because at the end of the day, a heritage brand isn't built on spreadsheets and exit strategies. It's built on relationships, integrity, design that lasts, and a refusal to sell your soul for a term sheet.

In a Nutshell

If I had to sum it up, building a company with misaligned capital is like inviting someone to help you build your dream home... and realizing halfway through that they'd really prefer a parking garage. There were moments of pure magic: Jennifer Garner's nursery in People Magazine, Bloomingdale's launching us in 17 stores, doubling revenue during a recession, and the first catalog landing in mailboxes. And there were also moments where I thought, "This is it. We're done"—investors threatening lawsuits, boardroom blowups over control, term sheets that required a magnifying glass and a stiff drink.

But here's what I learned in all of it:

- Capital is oxygen, but the wrong oxygen mask will still suffocate you.
- Saying no (even when you need the money) can be more powerful than saying yes.
- A handshake from someone who believes in you can be worth more than a million-dollar term sheet from someone who doesn't.
- Vision without capital is fantasy, but capital without vision is chaos.
- And most importantly: founders, not investors, are the ones who lose sleep, raise babies, ship boxes, and build brands.

We didn't always get it right. Some deals saved us. Others nearly broke us. Some days I celebrated. Others, I cried in my car before walking into the office. However, we stayed grounded in what mattered most: building a company with lasting value, treating people well, protecting the brand's spirit, and refusing to compromise our values for short-term gains.

In the end, that was what kept me going: the belief that success isn't just about revenue or valuation. It's being able to look your team, your family, and your investors in the eye and say, "We built this the right way. With integrity. With heart. And with just enough stubbornness to withstand the storms."

Reflection Questions

- When it comes to raising capital, what matters more to you, the money itself or who it comes from?
- Have you ever ignored your gut because the opportunity looked too good on paper? How did that turn out?
- What would you rather give up: control of your company, or speed of growth?
- How do you decide when to say *yes* to investors and when to walk away, even if the bank account is nearly empty?
- Have you ever experienced a partnership that looked perfect in a term sheet but felt wrong in real life? What were the signs you missed (or ignored)?
- What does "success" mean to you: a valuation, an exit, or being proud of how you got there?
- How do you protect your company's soul—its values, culture, and purpose—when outside money starts influencing decisions?
- When did you last pat yourself on the back for how far you've come, instead of focusing on the next crisis to fix?
- If it all went away tomorrow, would you be okay with how you built it?
- Who are the people who will tell you what you said when the noise gets loud, the chaos gets crazy, and the confusion gets real?

People: The Winning Formula

"Building a great team is less about hiring the best people, and more about creating the best environment for people to do their best work."
—Simon Sinek

The morning I realized we couldn't keep running the business on family and sheer willpower alone, I was standing in our tiny office surrounded by boxes, packing tape, and chaos masquerading as "early-stage entrepreneurship." Carina, my son Zeke's nanny, who later became a warehouse associate, was processing orders on the floor. Her sister, Evelyn, was sealing boxes like we were shipping gold. The printer jammed for the third time. My phone wouldn't stop buzzing.

Right then, it hit me—we didn't just need products or customers. We needed people. The right people. The kind who don't just clock in, but care. Building a business is never just about products. It's about community, trust, and bringing in people who make the dream real.

Your Winning Formula

One of the hard truths of entrepreneurship:

The team you need to go from zero to $5 million is not the same team that takes you to $50 million… or $500 million. It's unfair, uncomfortable, and absolutely true.

And yet, I'd be nowhere without the people who helped build Serena & Lily from scratch.

Carina Santos was first our nanny, and then our entire distribution center. Her sister, Evelyn, and another one of their buddies, Max, joined without question. The three of them shipped every package with such pride that you'd think they had signed each baby bumper themselves. Carina stayed with us for over 15 years and treated every order as if it were going directly to a VIP customer. Another early, exceptionally loyal operations employee was Gabi Avilles, who later came in 2008 and might still be at the company today.

Two of our very earliest hires were Shannon Flood and Mary Crofton, both of whom joined the company straight out of college. I'll never forget Mary walking in for her interview in a seersucker suit, complete with the most charming Southern accent and impeccable manners, all "yes ma'am" and "no ma'am." I vaguely remember her father calling to make sure we were a legitimate operation, which still makes me laugh. The idea of doing that to my own kids now feels cringingly painful, yet somehow also sweet in hindsight.

Shannon and Mary truly held up the entire business in those early years. They did everything: answering phones, entering orders, running trade shows, and tackling whatever else needed to get done. If it was essential, they handled it, and the company would not have survived those first few years without them.

When we finally admitted we needed actual operational expertise in 2010, we hired Dwight Nackord, a retired distribution center leader who probably thought he was coming in to consult for a few months. He stayed for more than eight years and quietly laid the foundation for a scalable business.

The lesson?

Sometimes your best hires don't come from résumés. They come from your network, the preschool parking lot, or the person packing boxes next to you who also happens to be brilliant.

The Creative Engine

If operations were the bones of Serena & Lily, the creative team was the soul—wild, colorful, opinionated, sleep-deprived, and absolutely brilliant. Serena to this day creates the most original pattern designs with a sensibility for color that I've never seen anywhere else. My home is filled with her most recent creations from her design firm, Serena Dugan Designs. From day one, we had Barb, a photo stylist with an eye for beauty and a trunk full of props that looked like they came from the most stylish flea market on earth. She could make a nursery look like a decorator showcase house. Barb worked with us as a freelancer for more than 14 years and helped create the visual language of our brand.

Then there was Satoko Furuta, our early creative director. She designed our catalogs like they were coffee table books. When she left for maternity leave and moved to Los Angeles, she only trusted one person to replace her: Frank Kofsuske, which says everything you need to know about Frank. He served as our Creative Director for over 8 years, a quirky and brilliant individual absolutely committed to translating Serena & Lily into imagery.

And then came Aaron Mutscheller, the "&" in Serena & Lily. He could float between the worlds of design and commercial translation without combusting, which is rare. Aaron led product design and development for around nine years, helping to translate creative ideas into actual, sellable products. He didn't just understand aesthetics; he understood how to turn it into a business.

They weren't just making pretty rooms.

They were creating a visual language, one that said: "Yes, you can have children *and* good taste."

Without them, we would've just been selling bedding. Instead, we built a brand.

The Multi-Talented Backbone

Every great company has a few people who quietly keep everything from hitting the floor. At Serena & Lily, we had the Karen Kiteas, Gigi Desin-Phillips, and Theresa Ramko, the unsung heroes who built the backbone of the business while the rest of us were running around chasing the next big idea.

Karen joined the customer care team early on, and twenty years plus, she's still there—cheerful, loyal, and probably the most relentlessly positive person on the planet. She set the standard for how we treated customers: with genuine warmth, not a script.

When the accounting became too much for me to handle as my side hustle, I hired Gigi as a part-time assistant controller. Within weeks, she was running accounting, payroll, operations, and, eventually, our distribution center. We called her our "Swiss Army knife." Every startup needs at least one.

Then came Theresa, who left Wall Street because she wanted to do something creative. She ultimately oversaw production, developed our inventory planning systems, and managed both wholesale and designer accounts. I always joked that she went from spreadsheets to duvets, but her financial discipline kept us from making many rookie mistakes. We hired Alison Heiland, a very scrappy production manager.

Our first adult supervision came in 2006 with Samara (Sam) Toole, our first marketing leader. She built everything from PR to our first e-commerce site. Before Sam, we'd sold exclusively wholesale for three and a half years. Her work flipped our business model and opened revenue channels that would eventually eclipse everything else. To this day, one of my fondest memories of being in a meeting with Sam was her repeated comment with her adorable, giggly voice, "We might just pull this thing off." Next came Brenda Scheumann, the next official "adult supervision." Fresh from the Gap, she brought process and structure to our product development chaos. When she spent her first month building a sourcing calendar instead of diving into the work, I panicked and thought I'd hired the wrong person. I soon learned she was building the foundation that would save us from countless disasters later.

Jan Leigner was our early Chief Operating Officer, and he rolled up his sleeves to partner closely with me on our first NetSuite implementation. By that point, the wheels were officially off the bus with our QuickBooks order management system. It could no longer handle a multi-user environment and was grinding to a complete standstill, literally freezing when someone hit the enter key.

These people didn't just wear multiple hats; they built the hat rack. They filled gaps we didn't even know existed, solved problems before we spotted them, and built systems from scratch that still supported the company years later.

Building Culture Through People

Some companies are built from spreadsheets and strategy decks. Ours was built from people, real people who cared about one another, showed up for each other, and made the office feel more like a community than a corporation.

When we hit about 30 employees, we hired Leigh Nikolaieff as our Head of People Success (HR felt too stodgy for what she actually did). I met her not in a boardroom, but at preschool drop-off. Our kids practically grew up together. She had 17 years of Human Resource experience at Williams Sonoma and knew structure, but she also knew soul. That combination was rare and exactly what we needed.

Leigh taught me to "put my hand on my heart" when making decisions about people. Not because it was sentimental, but because it ensured we never forgot the human side of business. She built everything, from our HR policies and onboarding processes to conflict resolution and exit procedures, always with dignity and compassion. She didn't just build systems. She built culture.

And culture wasn't a poster on the wall for us; it was how we lived inside the company:

- Halloween runway shows in the office (yes, executives included)
- Potluck lunches and baby showers where everyone showed up
- Traveling together to factories and trade shows and laughing until we cried
- Late-night catalog deadlines fueled by a bar cart and sheer adrenaline

Our customer care leader, Sam Robertson, used to coordinate entire themed costume acts for Halloween with his team. One year, Serena and I dressed as each other. One year, I dressed up with our Creative Director Frank as Pot Brownies, yes, Brownie uniforms, as in Girl Scouts with pot leaf patches, after all, we did build this company in the SF Bay area. That's when you know the culture is working.

There are a few additional people who were early team members who helped lay the foundation of this brand and shaped its heart and soul from the very beginning. Laurie Frankel, our extraordinary photographer, was a major ingredient in the secret sauce: her creative eye, her lighting, and her warmth helped define how the world first saw us. There was also Julie Mason, who developed the brand's voice through copywriting. Phil Neri, our scrappy CFO and true partner-in-crime, my "work husband," was by my side through every twist and turn as we ran around raising capital and willing this dream into reality.

Then there were our hilarious and wildly talented merchants, Kate Lesher and Katy Polsby, whose creativity and energy made every day a mix of laughter, chaos, and pure magic. And of course, Mike Donaldson, our sourcing guru and daily source of joy, who made me laugh every single day. Honestly, I'm not sure I could have made it through those 13 years without the laughter that was in our office in those days. Some other amazing and very loyal early team members, and this list could be so long, so this is pre 2011, or the team that has been so loyal to still be there today. I would be remiss not to shout out: Sarah Peterson, Laura Allen, Carla Rummo, Kirsty Williams, Carrie Crane, Tim Lewis, Chris Ritter, Sara Westover, Maura Nealon, Ivette Torres, Debra Magnani, Mary Randolph Norton, Kristin Merriman, Rick Ragusa, Eileen Grady, Kate Green, Stephanie Wu, Jessica Ecke, Rachel Merrill, Jennifer Crowley, Meg Meblin, Darby Asner, Wendy Wood, Cary Tiffin, Monica Gaspar, Gustavo Garcia, Sir Melvin Carter, and Steven Cox.

People worked hard. Really, really hard. But we also laughed hard. We cared about each other. And that closeness became our secret weapon. It held us together when investors caused chaos, when warehouses flooded, when boxes arrived crushed (again), and when everything felt like it could fall apart.

That kind of culture doesn't come from free snacks or mission statements. It comes from trust, respect, and showing up when it matters.

Teams Evolve

Here's something most founders don't talk about enough: the people who help you build a company from nothing are not always the same people you need to scale it to the next level. And that truth can break your heart a little.

As the company grew, the business's needs changed faster than some of the people inside it. The scrappy startup phase, where everyone wore 10 hats and figured things out on the fly, eventually gave way to the need for specialists, process builders, and leaders who had scaled from $50 million to $500 million.

But the tension was real:

- Institutional knowledge lives with your original team.
- Future growth often requires new deep expertise in a particular area.
- And loyalty makes those two realities collide.

Some say this is why founders can't lead companies past a certain size; they're simply too loyal to their people to make the hard calls. I understand that now.

By 2016, I was emotionally and physically exhausted. I'd been leading Serena & Lily for 13 years, through babies, rapid growth, capital raising, investor drama, all of it. I loved my team deeply. But I also knew the company needed different leadership for the next chapter. And I couldn't be the one to make the changes required while still honoring the people who built it with me.

In early 2014, I informed our newest investor that I was ready to hire a new CEO. He asked for a year to find the right person, which turned into eighteen months or more. At the end of 2015, the new CEO, Lori Greeley, stepped in, and I officially stepped out on December 31, 2015. That date didn't just mark my exit; it marked the end of the first era of Serena & Lily. Many of the original team left soon after. Not because they weren't loyal, but because the company had changed. Different leadership brought different vision, new processes, and new goals. And that's how it works. Painful, but true.

Was it easy? No.
Was it right? Yes.
Would I do it again? Only with better sleep and slowing down the growth.

This is one of the quiet heartbreaks of entrepreneurship: You build something like a family, and then, one day, you're asked to hire adults to run it.

Serena and I dressed up as one another for the Halloween runway show.

Serena and I distributed holiday gifts to our employees in 2013.

The Serena & Lily 10-year anniversary party under
the magic of the Golden Gate Bridge.

Summing It Up

Building a business is about strategy. Scaling a business is about people—the right people, at the right time, with the right kind of heart.

In the beginning, your team is made of believers. They're the ones who sit on the floor surrounded by shipping boxes, who do payroll at midnight, and who care as much about the dream as you do. They don't ask for titles or org charts. They ask, "What needs to get done?"

But as the business grows, so do the stakes and the skill sets required. You start needing systems, sourcing calendars, inventory planning, legal documents, HR policies, and people who actually know what a compliance audit is. That doesn't mean the early team wasn't amazing; it means they took you as far as they could. And that's something to honor, not hide.

I learned that my real job as a founder wasn't to do everything myself. It was to find extraordinary people and let them do what they did best:

- Serena's extreme point of distinction: original design.
- Barb's styling wizardry.
- Frank's quirky design vision.
- Aaron's design genius and design-to-dollars translation.
- Leigh's advice to put a hand over my heart when making decisions about people.

That was our secret sauce. Not the fabric. Not the catalog. Not even the business model. The people.

And when it was time for me to step away, it wasn't because I stopped believing. It was because I cared too much to stay in a role that no longer fit the company or my life. Leadership also means knowing when to hand the keys to someone else. Companies don't become heritage brands because of one visionary founder; they become heritage brands because of teams of people who pour themselves into something bigger than themselves.

Reflection Questions

- Who believed in your vision before it made sense on paper?
- What roles or skill sets does your business need now that it didn't need at the beginning?
- Are you keeping people in a role out of loyalty, even if the business has outgrown their responsibilities?
- How are you capturing institutional knowledge before it walks out the door?
- Could your culture survive without you?
- What's your real "secret sauce," and are you actively protecting and nurturing it?
- When would you know it's time to step aside or bring in new leadership?

CHAPTER 9

The Women Who Keep You Alive (and laughing) - A Sort of Survival Guide

This chapter is devoted to all the amazing women in my life who continue to show up for me. I am deeply appreciative, and your friendship means more to me than anything.

There are a few things I wish someone had told me a long time ago about being an adult. You know, like how there's no such thing as a quick coffee, how your calendar multiplies at an alarming rate the older you get, and that your friendships—especially the ones with your female friends—are actually a matter of life and death.

I'm not being too dramatic, I swear. I do have science on my side. For years, we've been treating friendships as some kind of fun little escape, a little treat we get to have once our careers, kids, and marriages are all sorted out. But the truth is, things don't just calm down once you hit your stride; they get a whole lot more hectic, stressful, and demanding.

And the truth I've finally lived long enough to say out loud is this: girlfriends aren't just a sprinkle on top—they're the foundation.

The Data - Because We Need to See the Stats to Believe It

For women specifically, Harvard researchers have found that women who are more socially integrated when they're in their midlife are more likely to live longer and make it to 85+, which is basically old. (Harvard Chan School of Public Health)

And to be honest, a lot of this seems to make sense. Even the American Psychological Association told us that stable friendships are linked to well-being and health all the way through life. (American Psychological Association) And if you're thinking, "Well, Duh—my friends are basically a well-being plan," then you get a gold star.

I still have a childhood friend, Cara Lee Krashin, from Kindergarten and my dear friend Eve Brosnahan from college.

Cara and I in college.

Eve and I while living together in Los Angeles post-college.

My friendships really deepened as I laid down my roots in Mill Valley for the past 27+ years.

Tina Sharkey: My BFF and neighbor

How Me and Tina Became Instant BFFs - A Crazy Story

My origin story with my BFF, Tina, feels like one of those only in hindsight do I get it moments—its all logistics and destiny wrapped up into one big coincidence. So, Tina was moving from New York to the Bay Area to take a CEO job at J&J's Baby Center, and her sister Lisa (who's also an extremely accomplished executive/connector) knew that Tina needed a soft landing and a strong community and connected Tina to Tiffany Shlain. And Tiffany - the great connector of all things female—knew just the right woman to plug Tina into: me.

We met for coffee at the Dipsea Cafe in Mill Valley, and let's just say we packed in what should have been six hours of conversation into 60 minutes. It was like speed dating for soulmates.

We talked about work, kids, our identities, marriage, ambition—you name it. It was the kind of conversation where you don't even bother with turns—we were in the zone. And when it was all said and done—after we'd basically crammed a years worth of conversations into one hour, Tina leaned back, took a breath and said her famous line: "I have to learn how to drive again, find a nanny, enroll my kids in school and start a new CEO job—can we just agree to be best friends so I can check it off of my to-do list?"

It was like she was checking off a box in her life. I didn't need to think about it. Yes, was my response.

That was it—that was the start of our lifelong friendship.

Me and Tina have a tradition—we throw the best birthday parties for our close friends every year. I mean, we really throw the parties—not just send out a birthday text with a balloon emoji. We create a whole birthday experience.

It's funny, it's healing to be celebrated by someone who knows your best chapters, your messy chapters, and all your other chapters, and still insists on a cake, candles, and a party for your loved ones. As adults, we become pretty cautious about asking for celebration—the kind of thing you'd normally want to throw a launch party or a fundraiser for, but suddenly, when we say "I'm having a birthday dinner" or "we need to celebrate this milestone," we start to feel like we're being a bit high-maintenance.

Tina's friendship made me realize that celebration isn't just for fun; it's a way of acknowledging and remembering the people in your life. It says: "You're still here, you matter, and we're taking a moment to appreciate our precious friendships."

And that's not all; it also has a really profound effect on your social network. These annual rituals create connections between people who might not otherwise have a reason to hang out. It makes friendship more of a community thing than just a one-on-one relationship.

Tina and I in Hawaii. She came out and helped me bake 12 challahs for a Christmas Shabbat dinner in 2020, serving 50 people. The first time people hung out in 9+ months, outside of course, and extremely memorable.

And here's the thing, being part of a community is actually really, really good for you. It's linked to better health, a better mood, a stronger immune system ... even a lower risk of dying (btw Public Library of Science (PLOS) looked into this).

Then there is Elana Rosen - the first friend who taught me to be a hope-a-holic

I met Elana 27 years ago, when I first moved to the San Francisco Bay Area. She was the kind of friend who didn't just roll out the welcome mat; she anchored you in the place.

Elana taught me a word I still love: hope-a-holic.

A hope-a-holic is someone who refuses to give up on the idea that things aren't always going to be horrific, even when all the facts are pointing in the other direction. It's not denial, it's not just being a positive thinker, it's a whole-hearted conviction that the story's not over yet.

Some people give advice, some people bring soup, some people bring perspective to the party ... Elana brings a load of hope and somehow she makes it her job.

What I've learned from her is that in marriage, you tend to have one person who's your main person, your partner who shows up for you. But in friendship, you get a whole chorus line of people who know you and can remind you of your own strengths.

Sometimes the best friend you can have is the one who comes along and says, "Hey, I know this version of you ... you've been here before, and you got through it, this too shall pass." That's not just comforting, that's actually pretty regulating for your nervous system.

We talk a lot about stress management, like meditation and supplements, but it's not just about those things; it's also about how we show up for one another. Through co-regulation and truth-telling, we can actually shift our biology in some really big ways.

Elana and I in Cambodia visiting Scott Neeson and the Cambodian Children's Fund in March 2024.

The marriage trap: expecting your spouse to do it all

Let's talk about husbands for a moment (with love). A lot of us were brought up on this idea that your spouse is your best friend, confidant, therapist, adventure buddy, intellectual sparring partner, emotional home ... yadda yadda yadda. And that is a heck of a lot to ask of one human being, especially when they're also a guy.

I love a good marriage, and honestly, I think they do better when they're not expected to shoulder every single emotional and conversational need.

There is a specific kind of relief when you stop trying to pour all your emotional baggage into one relationship, not because your partner isn't amazing, but because your life is complex and deserves more than one safe space to land.

Friends give you the space to be yourself, in all your messy, complicated, utterly human glory.

And the weird thing is, when you stop relying on your spouse to meet every emotional need, you sometimes end up showing up better in the relationship, less resentful, less depleted, less desperate for conversation.

Friendship is a practice - not a natural talent.

Some people say, "I'm just not good at keeping in touch," but that's not a personality thing; it's a habit you can build.

Friendship takes some effort, especially when you're juggling a million other things, a career, a family, a mortgage, an existential crisis at 2 a.m., etc.

The people who do this well aren't any less busy; they just appreciate that friendship isn't something you do after you've got your life sorted, it's actually a vital part of how you get through life.

I've learned to treat my friends like everything else in my life that matters, with a bit of structure. So I put a walk with my friends on the calendar, just like a meeting.

A weird thing happens when you put some structure in place: the good stuff starts to come out.

The holy trinity of a great friendship: laughter, having someone's back, and a healthy dose of truth.

If I had to boil down what my girlfriends have given me over the years, it boils down to three things:

Laughter.
Not that fake laugh that you just do out of politeness, but the kind of laugh that literally has you in tears, leaves you gasping for air, and needing a drink.

Having someone's back.
A friend who has watched you grow into who you are today, and still wants to sit in the front row for the next act.

Truth.
The kind of truth that's not mean-spirited or hurtful, but instead is honest and clarifies things when we need it. The kind of truth that says, "I've got your back, and I also think that's a pretty bad idea."

This is why having friends is so darn important. It's like having a steady supply of emotional truth spoken in a voice you trust.

A small nudge (that could change your life)

If you take one thing from this whole chapter, take this:

Your friendships need priority and nurturing, not because something's wrong, but because something's right, and it's really, really important.

Text the friend you've been missing lately. Make a plan before the week gets away from you. Start a new tradition. Be the one who organizes things and makes sure everyone shows up. Be the one who remembers everyone's birthdays.

And if you're waiting for permission to prioritize your girlfriends the way you do your job, your family, or your partner, well, consider this your permission slip, written with both your heart and the data.

Reflection questions

- Who are the three women you feel most like yourself around, and what is it about them that gets you?
- Where have you been relying too heavily on your spouse (or one person) for emotional stuff? What would it feel like to spread love around a bit?
- What friendship ritual could you start up that will make it impossible to ignore the others (monthly coffee, annual trip, weekly walk)?
- Who's the person in your life who always believes in a better tomorrow, and how can you be that person for someone else?
- If your friendships were a form of self-care, what appointment would you schedule this week to take care of them?

Raising Children While Building a Company

"Balance is not something you find,
it's something you create."
—Tory Burch (Founder of Tory Burch)

One Wednesday morning in 2008, I walked out of an investor meeting and straight into my middle son's kindergarten play. I was still in business clothes, heels clicking across the floor, surrounded by moms in yoga pants who'd been there since 8 a.m., organizing juice boxes and making small talk. The stares were ... not subtle.

But then my son peeked out from backstage, spotted me, and his whole face lit up. In that moment, every whisper, every judgment, every internal guilt trip faded. He saw me. That was enough.

Building a company and raising children taught me more than any boardroom ever could:

- A support system isn't optional; it's essential infrastructure.

- Consistency makes kids feel safe, even when life is chaotic.
- Quality time always beats quantity.
- Family traditions are anchors.
- Travel expands minds more than textbooks.
- Service teaches gratitude in a way lectures never can.
- You don't have to be at everything, just the things that matter.
- Independence is the greatest gift we can give our kids.
- Regret is normal; shame is optional.
- Every family needs its own recipe.

This chapter is my version of that recipe: the messy, beautiful, slightly chaotic formula that made it possible to build both a company and a family without losing my mind (most days).

The Village That Raised My Children

My life as a mom and entrepreneur started with one very honest realization: I couldn't do it all. The myth of the woman who runs a company, bakes banana bread, drives on every school field trip, keeps a spotless house, and looks rested? Fiction. Possibly science fiction.

So instead of chasing impossibility, I built a village.

Ingredient One: One Steady Caregiver from Day One

The first thing I did after having a baby wasn't write a business plan; it was hiring a full-time nanny. Not five rotating sitters, not a patchwork of friends and family, but one consistent person who would love and care for our child as we would. Children need routine, familiar faces, and people who genuinely care about them. That, to me, was non-negotiable.

Our nanny, Gladys Vasquez, became family. She still lives in an apartment on our property to this day. She loves our boys like they are her own children, the kind of love you can walk out the door and feel good about. I never left home worried. I left knowing my kids were safe and loved, with someone who knew their favorite stuffed animals and nap-time moods.

Gladys and I celebrating her birthday in 2025.

Ingredient Two: A Partner at Home Base

The second secret weapon was Marc on the ground. He handled doctor's appointments, field trips, school forms, sports registrations, all the things that get lost between investor pitch decks and shipping deadlines. He was a constant presence. I was a whirlwind.

To this day, I don't know how families manage when both parents have demanding corporate jobs in entirely different directions. Someone has to be the net, the one who catches everything that falls.

Ingredient Three: Backup for the Backup

With three boys under four, we always had a second nanny to support Gladys. Childcare was not a luxury item in our house; it was the oxygen mask. In lieu of fancy clothing, designer bags, or fancy cars, I invested in childcare. Not because I'm extravagant, but because peace of mind and emotionally secure kids were the foundation of everything else, including the company. I recognize this is not entirely accessible to every family, so I am grateful we had this luxury. I think the math came out close to my salary at the time.

So yes, I had help and a lot of it. And I make no apologies. Good childcare isn't a guilty indulgence; it's one of the smartest investments a working parent can make.

Ingredient Four: Family Dinner and Quality Time

The ingredient in my family and business survival recipe was simple: dinner together. Not every night, not with perfect table manners, and definitely not with gourmet meals—just dinner, at the table, together, most nights of the week. There's a lot of research indicating that family dinners are one of the strongest predictors of healthy kids—lower rates of anxiety, depression, substance abuse, eating disorders, early pregnancy; higher resilience, stronger vocabulary, better grades, and greater self-esteem. Harvard says so. But I didn't need the studies; I saw it in my boys.

Dinner was the one time of day when the phones were off the table. No email refresh, no investor drama, no last-minute fabric crisis. Just us.

We talked. Really talked. Highs and lows of the day. Moral debates inspired by world events. Occasionally, arguments over who was a better athlete. Some nights there were spills, sibling rivalry, and questionable jokes, but those nights were just as crucial as the peaceful ones. Because they were real, and real is what holds a family together more than perfectly folded napkins ever could.

I encouraged the same for my team. "Be home for dinner," I'd tell them. "The company will survive without you for an hour." I wanted them to know that work mattered, but not more than their people at home.

Ingredient Five: Family Vacations, Adventure as a Classroom

The fifth ingredient in our family formula was this: when life gets chaotic, get on a plane.

Not to a resort with matching robes and bottomless margaritas (though I fully support that kind of self-care), but to places where the world felt big, humbling, and honest. My husband, Marc, and I have always been wanderers. He lived in Zambia for five years, which meant Africa was the happy place destination for us; it was constantly calling us. So, when the kids were old enough to carry a backpack and sit on a long flight without crying (too much), we brought them too.

Christmas-time vacations became safaris in Botswana, fishing in Zambia, and jeep rides through Namibia's Skeleton Coast. Our boys learned to track lion footprints, negotiate with airport agents, and fall asleep in dusty Land Rovers somewhere between villages. They saw poverty and resilience co-exist in the most breathtaking views and the genuine awe of the natural world.

Serving lunch at an AIDS orphanage in Zambia.

One of the most meaningful experiences was serving lunch at an AIDS orphanage in Zambia. Over 60 kids, ages three to sixteen, sat quietly on the floor with their bowls, waiting for grace. They asked us to say the blessing, but all we knew was the *Motzi*, the Hebrew blessing over bread. So, we said it. In that moment, faith and service, Africa and Judaism, strangers and family, all blended in this beautiful, imperfect harmony. The gentleman who was the leader of that orphanage was in a wheelchair due to polio. Interestingly, at that time, Zambia was one of the few countries still affected by polio.

Ingredient Six: Learning Through Service

The sixth ingredient evolved naturally: if we were going to show our kids the world we wanted them to be in, we wanted them to be in service to it.

So, we built classrooms. Literally.

We dug foundations in Kenya's Maasai Mara. We made bricks in rural India. We worked shoulder-to-shoulder in Ecuador's Amazon. We took them to Kakuma Refugee Camp, home to over 300,000 displaced people from 25 countries. While Marc and I met with the heads of schools and hospitals, our kids played soccer with refugee children and taught them tic-tac-toe sitting on dirt floors.

Service wasn't about "saving" anyone. It was about understanding. It was about seeing how people with nothing could still offer hospitality, laughter, and strength. It made privilege visible, gratitude tangible, and compassion non-negotiable.

Some of our most chaotic memories are also our favorites: camping under stars in the Namib Desert with sand in everything, wild camping in Botswana, or the boys taking turns driving a stick-shift Land Rover across Zimbabwe while barely tall enough to see above the steering wheel.

Those trips didn't just bond us. They shaped our children's values more than any lecture ever could.

Ingredient Seven: Showing Up—Being Present for What Matters Most

The seventh ingredient in my parenting and entrepreneurship recipe was this: I couldn't be there for everything, but I made sure I was there for the things that mattered. I didn't make every practice, volunteer shift, or weekday field trip. Plenty of moms showed up with snacks and handmade props, while I arrived straight from supplier meetings, still wearing heels and a little out of breath. But I never missed the big stuff like school plays, teacher conferences, games, and all their friends' B'nai Mitzvahs.

One of my few real regrets is not carving out more one-on-one time with each child. I often convinced myself that if I couldn't give each of them equal time, then I wouldn't do it at all. I see now how wrong that math was—children don't need identical experiences; they need meaningful ones. They don't care if love is measured evenly, only that it is given fully.

Ingredient Eight: Love, Loss, and Modeling What Matters

The eighth ingredient was much quieter but just as important: modeling love, stability, and loyalty to family. When my mother became ill at the end of her life, I cared for her at our home while she was in hospice. It was exhausting and heartbreaking, but also, believe it or not, a true gift.

My boys watched me care for my mom with respect and tenderness. They saw that as much as I loved building a company, family came first. That's not something you can tell your kids. You have to model it; they are watching, not listening.

Ingredient Nine: Traditions That Ground You

The ninth ingredient? Ritual.

For us, it was Shabbat dinner. Every Friday night, no matter how chaotic the week was, we lit the candles, blessed the bread, and sat at the table together. Phones stayed off the table, and business talk remained off the menu. Most dinners were meaningful and spiritual, and we showed up week after week.

We hosted Shabbat dinners with families from each of our kids' classrooms, building community rather than just "playdate logistics." It wasn't perfect. It was real. And that was enough. I truly believed in the idea of everyone having a playdate at Shabbat dinners.

Ingredient Ten: Nurturing Independence—The Greatest Gift

The tenth ingredient in my parenting-and-entrepreneurship recipe was independence. Not the kind you talk about on parenting blogs—actual independence, the kind that makes other parents quietly question your judgment.

My kids learned to navigate airports before they could do simple math. They walked to town on their own, sold eggs around town in their wagon from our chicken coop, and figured out train routes better than I could. When our 13-year-old Zeke decided he wanted to climb Mount Kilimanjaro for his Bar Mitzvah, my husband offered to go with him. His response? "I want to do it alone." Most parents would've said no. We hired a local guide, made sure he had altitude medication... and let him go. He flew across Africa by himself, climbed six days to the summit, and came back on his own, a few years older in spirit. Other parents thought we were insane. Honestly, I'm still not sure we weren't.

But here's what I believe: kids don't become confident by watching us hold their hands. They become confident when we let go just enough for them to discover what they're capable of.

And yes, I was the "yes parent." At my 50th birthday dinner, our 9-year-old Nate gave a toast that began, "I love Mommy because when Dad says no, Mommy says yes." Was it a proud moment? Not exactly. Was it true? Absolutely.

Zeke at the summit of Kilimanjaro at 13 years old by himself on that adventure.

But nine years later, at 18, that same son stood up again and said: "My mom is the hardest working person I know, and she is kind to everyone she meets."

Independence isn't about letting your kids run wild. It's about trusting them to figure things out when you're not around to fix them.

Ingredient Eleven: Happy Parents

Last but not least, one of the most essential ingredients is a happy home with happy parents. This doesn't just happen; it takes work, serious work. This is an area my husband and I never took for granted; we worked on our marriage's happiness. We also made sure to reserve one night a week for date night. Kids aren't listening; they are watching.

In a Nutshell

Every parent-entrepreneur needs their own recipe. Mine worked for my life, a growing company, three sons, a husband who was self-employed and had a flexible work schedule, and the ability to invest in support. Your circumstances will be different, and so will your formula.

Here's what I learned:

- You can have it all, just not necessarily all on the same day.
- A strong support system isn't indulgent. It's essential infrastructure.
- Family dinners and rituals matter more than perfect attendance at every school event.

- Quality presence beats constant presence.
- Travel, service, and exposure to the broader world raise grounded, resilient kids.
- Independence is a gift and sometimes a leap of faith.
- Guilt is inevitable; perfection is not. Grace is essential.

My "ingredients" weren't perfect. I missed field trips and class volunteer days. I didn't always spend one-on-one time with each of my sons. I said yes too often out of guilt. But I also showed them purpose, passion, hard work, and what it looks like to build something with heart.

And one day, when my oldest son Max told me, "I never felt like I came second to your business," I realized—I must've gotten something right.

Because balance isn't about equal time; it's about being fully present where you are, when it matters. The smartphone came to market at the right time, which made my global journeys possible, so being fully present might be a slight exaggeration.

You don't have to choose between building a family and building a company. You just have to accept this truth: some moments/days belong to your business, some moments/days belong to your family, but your life belongs to both.

Reflection Questions

- What support system can you put in place now?
  (This could be a partner, nanny, grandparent, friend network, babysitting swap, or simply asking for help without guilt.)

- What are non-negotiables for you as a parent?
  (Is it bedtime? School plays? Friday night dinners? How will you protect them?)

- What family rituals or traditions can anchor your children, even when life is chaotic?
  (Sabbath, Sunday pancakes, family dinners, travel, storytelling, gratitude rituals, what feels real to you?)

- Where are you choosing guilt over practicality?
  (Are you trying to be everywhere instead of being fully present somewhere? What would it look like to choose presence over perfection?)

- How are you modeling resilience and independence for your children?
  (Do they see you solve problems? Take risks? Do you let them try and fail? What freedoms could you give them now that build confidence?)

- Are you raising kids who feel loved or kids who feel managed?
  (What small shifts could move your parenting from logistics to belonging?)

- When your children grow up, what do you most hope they will say they learned from watching you work and parent?

CHAPTER 11

The Adventures Where Memories Were Made

"There are experiences that leave footprints on your soul."
—Anonymous

People often assume that because I co-founded Serena & Lily, our family traveled in style in luxury hotels, infinity pools, and 500-thread-count sheets. And sure, don't get me wrong, I appreciate a nice lodge, especially now that we travel without the kids. But the truth is, the trips that gave us cherished family memories were the opposite of glamorous. They were gritty, unpredictable, outdoorsy, and full of moments that tested all of us in the best and funniest ways.

Those trips became our family's greatest stories, not because everything went perfectly, but because it absolutely didn't.

The Skeleton Coast: Where I Learned Toothpaste Is Not Shampoo

One of our all-time favorite family adventures was driving up the Skeleton Coast of Namibia with an outfit called Live the Journey. We camped for six nights, drove to the Angola border, and slept under stars and drove up and down very steep sand dunes, often getting extremely stuck in the sand. The kids were in rooftop tents, thrilled with the novelty of climbing into bed each night.

This was true wilderness. No hotels, no towns, no people except the nomadic Himba tribal people that live in that region. Just coastline, dunes, and desert animals like elephants and hyenas appearing out of nowhere.

And then there was the toothpaste incident.

Because we were only allocated one bucket of water each, I tried to be efficient and wash my hair quickly. I reached for what I thought was my shampoo; both were in similar reusable tubes, and I started lathering. Five seconds later, I realized I had fully washed my hair with toothpaste. Not a little. A full, minty lather from roots to ends.

I was so dirty, sticky, and I was exhausted. I cried. Our guide tried to be encouraging and said, "Don't worry, tomorrow night's camp has showers." We all clung to that hope.

We arrived the next night, desperate for hot water ... and the camp was out of it.

This is when the trip went from "adventure" to "family bonding exercise." Our son Zeke was so sweet and helpful, he offered to wash my hair using cold water as I lay back on a bench. That moment may have saved our marriage because I was one inconvenience away from completely losing it.

Camping in the sand dunes of Namibia.

On the Skeleton Coast of Namibia, at the site of an old shipwreck.

Botswana: The Moment I Nearly Divorced Marc

Another trip that lives in our family lore is the time we visited Elephant Sands in Botswana. To be clear, the bar area at Elephant Sands is one of the most magical places on earth. You sit there with a beer, and in front of you are what feels like 100 elephants crowded around a watering hole. You can watch them for hours. It's mesmerizing.

Then you go to your room.

Let's just say the accommodations feel like a very bad prison cell, minus the bars on the windows. I remember turning to Marc and thinking, "If I make it through this night, our marriage can survive anything." We laugh about it now, but in real time, I was mentally drafting the divorce papers.

Family Adventures Also Mean Family Misadventures

There was also the infamous Airbnb in the outskirts of Victoria Falls in Zambia, which we have since renamed the "Tarantula Inn." We lasted just barely 24 hours. When we were packing to leave, I went to close my suitcase, and a big furry tarantula sprinted out. I screamed, the kids screamed, and the tarantula sprinted underneath the refrigerator. I tried to capture the little furry monster on my iPhone, but unfortunately, my hand was shaking too uncontrollably.

Another highlight: the time we lifted the tarp of our tent in Mana Pools, Zimbabwe, and found a centipede curled up as if it had booked the space and was annoyed we were disturbing it. If you want to bond as a family, try dealing with unexpected wildlife inches from where you sleep.

Botswana, Zambia, and Malawi: Popcorn, Ferries, and Wild Camping

Despite (or because of) all these mishaps, our self-drives through Botswana, Zambia, and Malawi remain some of our favorite memories. We wild-camped in the Central Kalahari Game Reserve, made popcorn over a campfire, and lay under skies you cannot experience anywhere else.

We went tiger fishing on the Zambezi River, which Marc and the boys loved. I went along because, well, I'm just a good sport. And then there was the memorable 24-hour ferry across Lake Kariba. Not luxurious. Not comfortable. But you never forget it. On the other end of that journey, we stayed at a lodge on Lake Kariba called Rhino Lodge, where we met our favorite wildlife guide, Peter Tetlow. This guide could make you laugh every 5 minutes, and he was the most knowledgeable guide. He taught all the kids how to drive a stick shift in a Land Rover in the bush when they could barely see over the dash. He taught the kids how to track wild animal footprints. He also explained the entire civilization of a termite mound—wow, who knew? We have since that stay basically adopted Peter and his girlfriend, Kelly, as our travel companions. They are next-level fun!

We also drove across Madagascar, which is one of the most unusual and fascinating places on Earth. Everything about it, the unique lemurs, there are 100 different varieties of lemurs, the people are very unusual, with a mixture of Indonesian and African descent, and the architecture is also very unique.

Family photo in Zimbabwe

Tiger fishing on the Zambezi River.

A magical sundowner on Lake Kariba.

Marc and the boys stuck in mud in Zimbabwe with our dear friend Peter.

Gabon: A Long Walk, A Long Boat Ride, and Lowland Gorillas

One of our more intense expeditions was in Gabon with African Waters. The plan was simple: take a small internal aircraft to a remote fishing area on the Atlantic Ocean where it meets a river. What actually happened was not simple at all.

We arrived in Libreville to learn the plane had a mechanical issue. No one spoke English, and none of us spoke French, so we were piecing together information through hand gestures. What we did understand was this: the replacement plane couldn't take any additional weight, so our bags had to be driven to the lodge. Not exactly reassuring. Also, likely not the moment to pretend I weigh 10 pounds less than I do.

We were told we'd get our bags later the next night.

The Hospital Lunch and the Missionary Pilot

The next morning, they collected us for a four-hour drive to a tropical disease hospital to meet our replacement plane. Yes, a tropical disease hospital. And yes, the front entrance was literally a cemetery. We ate lunch there, doing everything possible to avoid getting stung by anything. We decided the mystery meat was probably pelican legs.

Then they drove us to the airstrip, where, surprise, our pilot was American. He was a missionary pilot for a hospital rescue organization. Before boarding the seven-seater, he had us all hold hands and say prayers, which is a very grounding experience when you're about to fly over dense rainforest.

In the air, everything was fine until it was time to land. He couldn't reach anyone on the radio. He simply said, "We need to land anyway because I need enough fuel to get back." Very calming.

We landed safely, boarded a boat for a few more hours down the river, and arrived at the lodge. If you ever want to meet the most eccentric, borderline-feral travelers on the planet, go to a remote fishing lodge in Gabon.

Lunch at the Hospital for Tropical Infectious Diseases,
enjoying our Pelican leg lunch.

Ladies in the back of the plane, myself and our son Max's girlfriend, Nicolette. I can still feel our nerves.

The Lost-Bag Meltdown

That evening, there were still no bags.

The lodge manager pulled us aside and said, very gently in a very French accent, "Your bags were in a terrible accident." She went on to say that when cars crash on rural roads, it's common for people to stop and steal whatever they can. At this point, I went into full-blown panic not for clothes or toiletries, but because all my hormone medications were in that bag.

I immediately grabbed my phone and started researching emergency exit flights out of Africa. Let's be honest: nobody wants to spend extended time with me when I'm off hormone replacement therapy.

They couldn't reach the driver, so the lodge manager's husband got in his car at night to go look for the vehicle. Hours passed. No updates.

Finally, around sunrise, the lodge manager returned with our bags. As it turns out, the van carrying them became the ambulance at the accident scene and spent the entire night driving the injured to a hospital. Miraculously, our bags were intact, and thankfully, there were no bloodstains. My hormone meds survived. Crisis averted.

The Remote Lodge, the Rain, and the Gorillas

After five nights of incredible fishing, plus getting drenched by rain every night, we packed up again.

From there, we hiked 20 kilometers through the rainforest and boarded another boat for a five-hour boat trip down the river to the lodge near the lowland gorilla area.

Seeing the gorillas made every chaotic moment worth it.

Was it exhausting? Yes. Would I do it again? Absolutely.

Fishing with African Waters Seta Cama in Gabon.

Fishing with African Waters Seta Cama in Gabon.

Service Trips: The Experiences That Grounded Us

Some of our most meaningful family trips were with WE.org (formerly Free the Children). Our family worked on classroom builds in the Maasai Mara in Kenya, in the rainforest of Ecuador, and in the mountains above Udaipur in India.

These trips weren't about tourism. We mixed cement, carried bricks, painted walls, and connected with local families. We learned firsthand what all the issues were that impacted these remote villages around the world, from clean water, education, medical clinics, and sustainable trades. We.org ran the largest artisan group of women Masai beaders.

Building a classroom in the Masai Mara in Kenya.

Building a classroom in the Masai Mara in Kenya.

Building a classroom in the mountains above Udaipur, India.

Service trip in the Amazon Rain Forest in Ecuador.

Cambodia: A Family Milestone

Most recently, we traveled to Phnom Penh to dedicate a climbing wall at Cambodia Children's Fund, which our son Zeke managed and helped build. Being there, meeting the kids, and seeing the difference the organization makes was deeply moving.

Dedicating the climbing wall in Cambodia at the Cambodian Children's Fund with my husband Marc, our sons Zeke and Nate, and my 88-year-old mother-in-law, Inge.

The initial climbing club at the Cambodian Children's Fund.

And I'll repeat this wherever I can: sponsor a child if you can. It's $150 a month. It changes a life. You have a pen pal relationship, and visiting in person takes that understanding to an entirely new level.

Why These Trips Matter

Not one of our most meaningful trips involved a fancy hotel. They were messy, funny, sometimes uncomfortable, and always memorable. They made our boys adaptable, curious, and grounded. They brought us closer together, even when a tarantula was sprinting out of my suitcase or I was contemplating divorce at Elephant Sands.

They taught us that the best family memories often come from the unexpected moments, the challenges, the mishaps, the teamwork, the laughter afterward.

Those are the stories we still tell.

Reflection Questions

- What are the trips your family still talks about?
- Were they perfect, or were they imperfect in the best possible way?
- What kind of adventure or service trip could you imagine doing next?
- What story do you want your children to remember about your time together?
- How might you step just a little outside your comfort zone for the sake of connection?

CHAPTER 12

Doors Open and Doors Close

"We need to accept that we won't always make the right decisions, that we'll screw up royally sometimes — understanding that failure is not the opposite of success, it's part of success."
—Arianna Huffington (Founder, Huffington Post; Thrive Global)

Standing in our first Serena & Lily retail store in the Hamptons one August morning in 2013, I watched a well-dressed stranger linger a little too long. He wasn't shopping. He was studying. After about five minutes, he approached our store manager and asked, "I'm here to meet Lily."

I was somewhere between Africa and New York when I received the text that a man had come into the store and asked to meet the founders. He turned out to be a potential investor who had been given a simple directive from his financial backers: find a company worth acquiring a majority interest, and we'll back you with the capital to take control.

What still amazes me is how the biggest turning points in life tend to appear in the most ordinary of circumstances. No announcement, no warning. Just a guy wandering in our store in the Hamptons.

That quiet visit would kick off a series of decisions that would reshape my professional life, test my family, and ultimately bring me closer to my purpose.

Here's what I learned during the years that followed:

- Every door that closes is usually protecting a better one you haven't seen yet.
- Success gives you choices, but choices require courage.
- Business crises and personal crises often arrive hand in hand.
- The right partner can resurrect a dream; the wrong one can suffocate it.
- Sometimes the bravest move isn't fighting harder; it's letting go.
- True wealth is being able to choose meaningful work, not just making things bigger.
- Legacy matters more than valuation.
- Reinvention gets easier when you trust your superpowers.
- Community can carry you when ego and ambition can't.
- The move from success to significance doesn't happen by accident; it happens by choice.

This chapter is about the doors that opened, the ones that slammed shut, and the surprising hallways in between, from selling a controlling stake in Serena & Lily to launching new ventures, from caring for my mother in hospice during a pandemic to building an interior design studio in Hawaii. Each twist revealed something more profound about what truly matters when the noise settles.

The Hamptons Store Success That Changed Everything

After turning down earlier acquisition offers because of our complicated capital structure, Serena and I did what we've always done best: we doubled down and got back to work. If investors wouldn't value our brand the way we did, we'd show them why they were wrong.

So, we opened our first Serena & Lily retail store in the Hamptons. It was exactly where our customer shopped, summered, and entertained. It was also where many New York-based consumer investors spent their weekends, which didn't hurt.

We opened the doors in June 2013, just in time for summer. By August, the well-dressed stranger walked in.

Over lunch a few days later, he told me something that warmed my heart: he had heard a consumer consulting presentation on consumer brands to watch, and Serena & Lily was on the list. He was interested in exploring a majority investment. Not only that. He would also help us fix the one thing blocking our growth— our messy capitalization table.

His proposal sounded like a miracle:

- Buy out the investors who wanted to exit.

- Convert the rest to common stock.
- Create a single class of shares, with founders, employees, and new investors all aligned in a single class of stock.

This was precisely the kind of capital restructuring we'd dreamed of but didn't completely know how to make happen.

And just when we needed it most, the universe sent another gift: a woman named Carla Rummo walked into our office, résumé in hand, having recently left private equity and looking for an operations role at a brand she admired. I hired her part-time to help us manage this deal, with the option to join full-time if it closed.

She was brilliant—Ivy League undergrad, Stanford MBA, fluent in private equity, waterfalls, and diplomacy. With her help, investor negotiations made sense. After months of structuring, negotiating, and compromise from every side, the deal closed.

We finally had what we fought for:

- A clean cap table
- Majority investment from one partner
- A path forward, funded and simplified

But, like most wins in business, it came with a cost—one that would force me to make one of the hardest decisions of my career.

The Difficult Choice: Selling Majority Ownership

When the deal closed, most people, including my eleven-year-old son, asked the same question:

"Why would you sell majority control of your own company?"

The answer was painfully simple: we didn't have a choice. Our capital structure had become so convoluted with liquidation preferences and multiple layers of investors that we were officially deemed "uninvestable." Without restructuring and fresh capital, we couldn't grow. Worse, we might not survive.

Looking back, if I could redo one thing at that moment, it's this: I would have hired separate legal counsel for Serena and me personally.

Our corporate attorney advised it. But we were exhausted, financially stretched, and honestly very trusting. We believed everyone around the table had good intentions. We wanted the deal to work so badly, we didn't protect ourselves the way we should have.

And we were tired.

We hadn't taken big salaries in years. We'd been living off savings. The finish line felt close, and I didn't have the emotional bandwidth for another legal ordeal.

Once the deal was done, I was utterly depleted.

After sprinting for over a decade without stopping to breathe or celebrate, I told our new majority investor that it was time to find a CEO to take the company into its next phase. He asked for a year. I gave him over eighteen months.

We eventually recruited a phenomenal consumer leader, Lori Greeley, a true merchant builder who loved Serena & Lily as much as we did. She first joined our board, then stepped into the CEO role.

On December 31, 2015, I officially stepped down as CEO.

But I've never been very good at staying still.

After decompressing for 18 months, a new opportunity appeared, one that combined business, philanthropy, and purpose in a way I'd been dreaming about for years.

From Decompression to New Purpose: Boon Supply

After stepping down as CEO, I stayed on the board, took eighteen months to decompress, and tried to remember what it felt like to sleep without waking up in a cold sweat thinking about inventory or investor calls.

Then an opportunity landed in my lap.

A friend, Jill Horn, approached me about buying a merchandise-based school fundraising company. It wasn't glamorous—think reusable grocery bags and gift wrap sold through school catalogs—but it was doing very good for the world. Over $75 million had already been given back to schools and nonprofits.

And instantly something lit up inside me. Back in 2008, I sat in a Henry Crown Fellowship program at the Aspen Institute and listened to my classmate, Tamsin Smith, talk about how she helped launch the (RED) Campaign, the one that raised hundreds of millions of dollars for the Global Fund for AIDS through everyday consumer brand partnerships. That idea stuck in my brain for many years: what if shopping could fund change? What if buying beautiful, everyday things could do good in the world?

So, in May 2017, with the help of a few investors, we bought the company.

We renamed it Boon Supply and launched in early 2018.

We rebuilt everything: the brand, the technology, the merchandise assortment, the catalog creative, and the mission. We layered a GoFundMe-style platform on top of Shopify so anyone could launch a fundraiser for their school, team sport, or any cause. Fifty percent of every purchase went directly back to that fundraiser.

The first two years were stunning:

- $44 million in revenue.
- $22 million donated back to schools and nonprofits.
- Momentum, heart, and mission all working in perfect harmony; it was an exciting innovation.

And then just when it felt like everything was finally aligned...

The world stopped.

When Everything Falls Apart at Once

We all know what happened next: March 2020 arrived, and the world shut down.

Overnight, our entire business model collapsed. Schools closed. Sports games were canceled. No bake sales, no PTA meetings, no catalog fundraisers. And our Shopify dashboard looked like a flatline; we went to nearly zero revenue, like someone had unplugged the company from life support.

We had:

- 24 employees
- A warehouse full of inventory purchased for a $10M spring season
- Almost no cash reserves

Within weeks, I had to lay off a lot of our staff. It was brutal.

We applied for PPP loans and attempted to figure out how to liquidate millions of dollars in inventory just to stay afloat. My brilliant and extremely capable Chief Revenue Officer, Christina Snyder, reached out to *Good Morning America Deals & Steals*. Tori Johnson shared our story with heart and urgency, and in 48 hours, we did $1 million in sales. Not profitable, but enough cash to breathe. Enough to stay in the game.

And while all of that was happening, life threw something even harder my way.

In late 2019, my mom went into hospice care. I moved her from Kansas City to live with us in Mill Valley. We hired 24-hour caregivers. I knew time was short. COVID killed my business. But COVID also gave me one of the greatest gifts of my life: quality time with my mother, who was in her final months of life.

We were all home. Every meal together. No travel. No boardrooms. No distractions. I could not have asked for a bigger gift to spend quality time with my adorable and sweet mom.

She sadly passed away in May 2020.

Boon Supply limped along for the rest of the year. A few schools reopened. But fundraising never went back to what it was. My mom was gone. The business was hemorrhaging. And I was exhausted in ways I never knew existed.

That time period taught me something I will never forget:

Sometimes everything falls apart, not to break you, but to clear the space for what matters most.

The Great Escape: Finding Paradise Amid Crisis

By August 2020, after losing my mom, watching Boon Supply collapse, and living through a global pandemic, I was done.

So, we did something crazy: we moved to the Big Island of Hawaii, so our two younger sons could attend high school in person. No more Zoom classrooms, no more isolation. Just a fresh start, ocean air, and a slower pace of life.

And honestly? It was one of the best decisions we ever made.

- The boys thrived at Hawaii Preparatory Academy.
- We met kind, down-to-earth people who became lifelong friends.
- The island gave us space to heal, think, and finally breathe.

During that time, I tried to revive Boon Supply. I even raised a small round of funding because I still believed in it—commerce for good, fundraising for schools.

But the business model had changed. Completely.

The entire system depended on school-based fundraising reps, most of whom were commission-only reps who had moved on to other jobs during COVID or retired. They didn't come back. Schools were burned out. Budgets were cut. And fundraising, as we knew it, just didn't bounce back.

I had to face the truth:

We couldn't get the business back to scale. The economics were broken. And no amount of grit or optimism was going to fix it.

So, I made one of the hardest decisions of my career:

I shut it down.

Not because I didn't love it.
Not because it didn't matter.
But because it was time to stop pouring energy into something the world had outgrown.

The school fundraising industry, as it existed before the COVID-19 pandemic, never really recovered. And I had to accept that.

But here's the surprising part: closing the business didn't feel like failure. It felt like freedom. Like finishing a chapter I was never meant to live in forever.

Endings are painful, but they create space for beginnings.

Full Circle: The Serena & Lily Exit

Around the same time we were winding down Boon Supply, another door opened, one I didn't expect.

Serena & Lily, the company Serena and I had poured nearly two decades of our lives into, put together a tender offer to buy out any early investors or employees who wanted liquidity. It was not completely clear at the time, but later it became clear that the lead investor was preparing the company for an IPO. To do that, they needed to clean up the capitalization table, which meant giving early shareholders, friends-and-family investors, former employees, and founders like me the option to fully cash out. There was one rule: sell all your shares, or sell none—no half-steps.

Marc and I sat with the question: How much is enough?

Financially, we already had what anyone could reasonably want: security, a home we loved, the ability to educate our children, and to give back to causes we care about. My dream has always been to one day donate $1 million a year to causes I care about. This exit offer didn't get us anywhere near that goal, but it got us comfortable with what we had and the ability to give back modestly to causes we cared about, and continue to follow our passions.

So we made the decision.

We sold.

Not because we stopped believing in the company, but because it was time. Eighteen years is a long time to carry the weight of something you built. It was time to let it go and let it fly without me.

We bought a home in Hawaii as a quiet reward for all the years of grit, sacrifice, and unbelievable effort. I truly believed we would live there full-time and raise our boys through high school, grow roots in the sand, and never look back.

Our California property became a rental and a long-term safety net.

We were ready for the next chapter.

Of course, life being what it is, the next chapter didn't look anything like we expected. It rarely does.

New Creative Ventures: Averylily Design Studio

When we settled into Hawaii, I did what any design-obsessed entrepreneur does: I asked to meet the interior designer of the home we had just purchased. In Hawaii, you often buy homes fully furnished, because shipping a sofa across the Pacific isn't the easiest or most timely thing to do.

That's how I met Avery Solmssen.

She was thoughtful, talented, and had this effortless style that felt like Hawaii—natural, soulful, and unpretentious. We began working together to add a little more color and texture to the house. One pillow turned into wallpaper. One wallpaper turned into a custom Hawaiian-style pune'e (local version of a daybed). And soon enough, we were dreaming way beyond pops of color.

One day, I asked what I thought was a harmless question: "Why haven't you started your own design firm?"

She hesitated. She wasn't sure she was ready to do it alone.

So I said, "What if I did it with you?" I became her first investor and partner. No big pitch deck, no board meeting, just two women who shared a love of beauty, craftsmanship, and creating spaces that feel like home.

We launched our interior design business in late summer 2022.

It happened the way the best ideas do, organically, joyfully, and a little bit chaotically.

That August, we traveled to Cape Town, South Africa, gathering ideas, textiles, and inspiration from artisans and makers. It was the closest thing to magic I'd felt in a long time. Two creative women, new business partners, eating at too many delicious restaurants and talking late into the night about design, purpose, and life.

We toyed with calling the business Studio A.L., but our branding logo development team said, "You'd be crazy not to use both of your names." And so there you have it—Averylily was born.

Soon after launching:

- All of Avery's long-time clients followed her to the new company.
- We introduced our own bedding, bath, and beach collection in early 2024.
- We're currently developing a signature fabric line, inspired by Hawaii and global artisan traditions.
- And yes, we're dreaming about a flagship store in Hawaii... and maybe California.

In this period of my life, creating beauty feels less like business and more like soul work.

Interior design was the first language I ever truly spoke, long before spreadsheets, investors, or board meetings. Coming back to it feels like coming home.

Avery and I at our launch party of Averylily in our offices in Honolulu.

One of the best souvenirs of our Hawaii getaway is the most adorable and sweet
Pit Bull mix rescue named Rock. I call him our Pit Bunny.

The lessons I learned on my journey

Whenever someone asks whether I made big mistakes along the way, I usually laugh and say I could write a five-hundred-page book on that topic alone. The truth is, mistakes are not the exception in entrepreneurship; they are a given. But the ones that mattered most, the ones that left a lasting imprint, can be distilled into a handful of lessons I wish I had learned earlier.

The first was misaligned capital.

Businesses that require inventory and meaningful working capital are often a poor fit for Silicon Valley-style technology investors or any venture capital model built for rapid, capital-light scaling. In these businesses, growth is not accretive. The faster you grow, the more capital you consume. Until you have several years of profitability, access to a line of credit is limited, which means growth is funded almost entirely through equity. That cycle can be brutally dilutive not just for founders, but for employees and early believers who helped get the company off the ground.

The second mistake was raising capital only when we needed it.

Urgency clouds judgment. We found ourselves taking money from investors I instinctively knew were not the right partners. When you are under pressure, you convince yourself that capital is neutral, that money is money. It isn't. The wrong investors don't just affect your cap table; they affect decision-making, culture, and your own sense of agency as a leader.

The third lesson was about terms, not valuation.

For too long, I focused on headline valuation rather than insisting on clean, balanced terms. That was a costly mistake. Liquidation preferences, control provisions, and structural complexity often matter far more than price. A "great" valuation with bad terms undermines years of hard work.

The fourth was title inflation in the early days.

Handing out Vice President or C-suite titles when a company is between zero and ten million dollars in revenue rarely ends well.

What a company needs from its leaders changes dramatically as it grows, especially in an omnichannel consumer brand. Titles given too early can become constraints later, making necessary evolution feel personal instead of strategic. Technology companies may play by different rules, but in consumer businesses, this lesson is non-negotiable.

Another, deeper area of learning was knowing when to let go and not doing it soon enough.
When COVID effectively destroyed Boon Supply, I tried to bring it back anyway. I chased a business that was clearly finished, convinced I could crack the code and put it back on track. Every signal told me it was over, but I wasn't ready to listen.

In hindsight, I can see how much of that persistence was driven by ego, by my unwillingness to accept that something I built with so much heart had failed. Letting it go felt like admitting something about myself that I wasn't yet prepared to face.

What I feel I got right, and would not change if I did it all over again.
I wouldn't change the way I showed up. I built an extraordinary company culture. I believe I led with transparency and integrity, even when the answers were unclear. I partnered with an exceptionally talented creative and design leader in Serena. And I made the decision to step aside as CEO at exactly the right moment.

I knew my superpowers had reached their natural limit. The company needed a different kind of leadership to reach its next phase, and I trusted that truth even though it was uncomfortable.

I believe wholeheartedly that making that transition when I did gave the business its greatest possible chance to become something truly significant.

Here is what I understand now:

What I understand now is this: ego isn't always loud or obvious. Sometimes it disguises itself as grit, as loyalty to the thing you built, as the refusal to walk away. Identity can become so tightly woven into our work that ending a chapter feels like erasing ourselves. Leadership maturity is learning to separate who you are from what you've built and recognizing when the work is no longer about saving a business, but about evolving yourself. Letting go didn't mark an ending for me; it created the space for reinvention. And in that space, a deeper question emerged, one that would guide everything that followed: If success is no longer the goal, what kind of impact do I want to make next?

Looking Ahead: Legacy and Influence

Reaching this phase of life means asking different questions, not *What's next?* but *What will matter most when it's all said and done?*

Legacy starts to matter, not in a dramatic, ego-driven way, but in a quiet inventory-taking of your gifts, your energy, and what you want to leave behind.

I've learned to ask myself:

- What are my true superpowers?
- How can I use them to make the world a little better than I found it?

- What does moving from success to significance really look like?

For me, it's a combination of family, creativity, community, heart, and design—the threads that have always run through my life, no matter the job title. I'm trying to spend more time with my family now, at least as much as my young adult sons still allow me. We still try to take one big family trip every year, but coordinating the schedules of five adults is a full-time logistics puzzle. I also love gathering everyone for our annual Passover Seder, which for us is the equivalent of Christmas dinner—storytelling, ritual, laughter, and a little chaos.

Meanwhile, the world feels politically, socially, and morally unpredictable. Some days it feels like we're living in a global identity crisis. I worry about the next generation, how much unrest and uncertainty they're absorbing, and how social media is shaping their understanding of truth and belonging.

It's tempting to disengage, but I believe more than ever that we need clear-eyed, compassionate, grounded leadership. Not louder voices... wiser ones.

Selecting Work That Matters

Given all that, I've become careful about where I invest my time.

Here's my litmus test now:

- Does this align with my values?
- Does it support community, dignity, creativity, or opportunity for others?
- Will this help leave the world better or just busier?

That's why I've chosen to serve on boards focused on humanitarian aid and community-building rather than politics. I've lived long enough to know that innocent civilians pay the highest price in conflict. I choose work that alleviates suffering, not debates about who's winning.

As a daughter of Jewish grandparents who survived Eastern European antisemitism and the trauma of the Holocaust, I cannot ignore what is happening to the Jewish people globally today. I feel a responsibility not just to speak up, but to help, to build, to connect, to keep the community strong.

Investing in Artisans and Women

The second great love of my life, after family and community, is elevating the work of global artisans, especially women, and helping them earn a dignified income. These craftspeople are masters of techniques passed down for generations, yet often live on the margins of global commerce.

Bringing their work to the world isn't charity; it's pure magic and collaboration. It's business with a soul. And it's one of the most fulfilling intersections of my skills and passions.

Empower Her: Philanthropy Meets Investment

Along these lines, I co-founded with Beth Stelluto a collective called Empower Her, an impact investment fund built on the idea that philanthropic capital can do more than sit in a Donor Advised Fund; it can be put to work within companies, solving real humanitarian or environmental problems. We invest in "for-profit" companies that deliver double-bottom-line results, profit and purpose. At the time of writing, we've invested in six companies that align with that vision. This model is built on top of CataCap.org, an absolutely brilliant innovation created by Tim Freundlich and Ken Kurtzig.

Summing It Up

If there's one thing life has taught me, it's this: doors don't stay open forever. Some you walk through, some you close behind you, and others slam shut while you're still standing in the doorway, wondering what just happened.

Since 2016, my life has been one long hallway of doors: Serena & Lily, Boon Supply, my mother's final chapter, Hawaii, Averylily, and now this next season of purpose, creativity, and legacy.

Some of what I learned along the way:

- Sometimes, selling your company is not a glamorous exit story; it's survival, strategy, or simply the next right thing.
- Letting go is not failure. It makes space for what's next.
- Two things can be true at once: my business collapsed, and I got the gift of being with my mother in her last months.
- Success and heartbreak don't happen in sequence; they often arrive on the same day.
- Reinvention isn't about starting over; it's about returning to who you've always been.
- Money gives you comfort and freedom. Purpose gives you oxygen. You need both.
- Legacy is not what you build. It's what lives on in people because of you.

Selling Serena & Lily felt like the end of a dream, but it gave me the freedom to start new ones. Boon Supply fell apart, but it gave me time with my mother, which I would never trade. Moving to Hawaii healed something in me I didn't know was broken. Launching Averylily reminded me: I am still a builder, still a designer, still a founder, just doing it with more wisdom, less ego, and a lot of sunshine.

The most significant shift of all has been this: for most of my life, I chased success. Now I chase significance. I no longer want to just create beautiful products. I want to create beauty, dignity, and opportunity in people's lives, in communities, in the world.

Because in the end, businesses get sold, companies go public or go bankrupt, trends fade, and houses change. But the way you showed up for your people, your purpose, your family, your convictions that stay, and that is how you will be remembered.

Reflection Questions

- Which doors in your life felt like endings but were actually beginnings?
  (Can you see them differently now?)
- How do you define "enough" for yourself financially, emotionally, and creatively?
  (Are you living by your own definition or someone else's?)
- Have you ever walked away from something successful because it no longer aligned with your values or well-being?
  (What gave you the courage, or what held you back?)

- What is legacy to you?
  (Wealth, impact, family, faith, creativity, or something else?)
- When life forced two big things to happen at once (business crisis and personal crisis), how did you respond? (What surprised you about yourself?)
- What parts of you remain steady through every transition? (The constants beneath all the titles, roles, and business cards.)
- Who are the people or communities that keep you grounded when everything else shifts?
  (How are you nurturing those relationships?)
- What strengths, gifts, or superpowers do you want to use in this next period of life for impact, joy, or service?

CHAPTER 13

A World on Fire and Why I Still Believe

"I call myself a hope-a-holic, and here's why."
—Lily Kanter

This morning, I woke up, waiting for my coffee to finish brewing, doom-scrolling headlines like so many of us do:

- Another spike in teen depression
- Another report about families who can't make ends meet
- Another conflict somewhere in the world that feels impossibly far from resolution
- Another mass shooting

If you're paying attention, it's hard not to feel the weight of it all pressing down on your shoulders.

But here's what building a business and raising three boys taught me about hope: even when the world looks like it's on fire, there are always people quietly choosing to build something better.

This chapter isn't about ignoring what's broken. It's about looking at the mess honestly and still choosing to believe, choosing to act.

These are lessons for anyone who is:

- Trying to raise grounded kids in an ungrounded world
- Wondering if business can still be a force for good
- Holding onto hope when cynicism would be easier
- Wanting to contribute to solutions, but not sure where to start
- Learning how to care about the world while also protecting your inner peace

Yes, the statistics are sobering. The headlines are heavy. But they aren't the whole story. We are also living in a time where individuals have more power than ever before to do good.

The Weight of Our Times

We're living in a time of staggering contradictions. On the one hand, humanity has never been more advanced. On the other hand, so many people feel completely lost and more polarized.

Teen mental health is in crisis, especially for girls. The CDC reported that in 2023, 53% of high school girls felt persistently sad or hopeless, double the rate a decade earlier. And it's not just girls. Boys aren't okay either. Anxiety, isolation, and screen addiction are shaping an entire generation. The average teenage boy now spends over eight hours a day staring at a screen, much of it fed by algorithms selling violence, disconnection, or a warped version of masculinity.

The American Dream? For many, it feels like it's slipping away. Over 60% of Americans live paycheck to paycheck. Even families with two incomes are struggling to afford housing, groceries, college, and childcare. People are working harder than ever and still feel like they're falling behind. Instead of bringing us together, technology is dividing us. Social media doesn't just show us the world; it edits it, filters it, and feeds us only what we already agree with. It's brilliant at selling outrage. A 2024 Pew study found that most Americans believe social media is doing more harm than good to our society. You can feel it in politics, schools, dinner tables, and friend groups.

Globally, the problems feel even bigger. Conflict, famine, and displacement have increased; more people rely on humanitarian aid today than at any other time in history. Yet American support is shrinking. In places like Ukraine, Gaza, Sudan, and the Horn of Africa, the absence of aid isn't political; it's life or death.

And then there's the painful rise of antisemitism. As a Jewish woman, seeing synagogues vandalized, mass murders in Washington, DC, Boulder, and Bondi Beach in Australia. Jewish students threatened, and conspiracy theories spread openly, is frightening. The Anti-Defamation League reported an 893% increase in antisemitic incidents in the past decade, the highest ever recorded. Things our grandparents said would "never happen again" are happening again in plain sight.

But the thing about statistics is they only tell us what's broken, not what's possible.

And what's possible is still extraordinary.

The Global Perspective

If the challenges at home feel overwhelming, a look at the global landscape can make them seem even more daunting.

More than 360 million people worldwide now rely on humanitarian aid just to survive, for food, clean water, medicine, and shelter. Yet U.S. support for international aid has fallen below 0.2% of GDP, well short of the commitments we've historically made to the world.

At the same time, distrust in capitalism and Western institutions is growing, especially among younger generations. Many don't see capitalism as a system of opportunity anymore, but one of inequality, unchecked greed, and environmental destruction. In one survey, less than half of Gen Z said they viewed capitalism favorably, and nearly as many said they preferred socialism. And while some of their critiques are valid, what worries me is how easily the narrative becomes black and white: West equals oppression. Capitalism equals greed. Tradition equals injustice.

What gets lost is the nuance, the fact that these same systems have also lifted billions out of poverty, created life-saving medicines, expanded human rights, and built the very freedoms we now use to criticize them. This isn't to say everything is fine. It's not. But if we only see the flaws, we risk teaching a generation to dismantle systems without understanding how to rebuild something better.

These global challenges are real. They justify fear, anger, and exhaustion.

But they are not the whole story.

While aid budgets shrink, people still show up in disaster zones. While hate rises, communities are forming to fight it. While faith in institutions weakens, individuals and small organizations are quietly rebuilding trust from the ground up.

Which brings me to why I still call myself a hope-a-holic.

Why I'm Still a Hope-a-holic

With everything happening in the world, people often ask me, "How can you still be optimistic?"

Because the other half of the story, the one that rarely makes headlines, is just as real:

- Global hunger has fallen dramatically. In 1990, nearly 1 in 5 people worldwide were undernourished. Today, that number is under 9%. (World Health Organization)
- Children are surviving. Infant mortality has dropped by more than 50% worldwide since 1990, thanks to vaccines, maternal health care, and basic sanitation. (World Bank)
- Education is spreading. Over 93% of young people aged 15-24 worldwide can now read and write. (UNESCO)
- Diseases that crippled generations, polio, malaria, and HIV, are being eradicated or controlled at unprecedented rates.
- More people than ever live in democratic societies with access to speech, voting, the rule of law, and opportunity.
- Technology democratized entrepreneurship. With nothing more than Wi-Fi, a laptop, and courage, millions of people, especially women, can now earn their own

income, start businesses, or support their families from anywhere in the world.

- Women are rising. More women than ever before are leading governments, launching companies, sitting on boards, and running Fortune 500 companies, more than at any other point in history.

These things didn't just "happen." They were built by innovators, activists, entrepreneurs, philanthropists, and dreamers who refused to believe the world was doomed.

That's why I'm a hope-a-holic.

Not because I'm naive.

Not because I ignore the darkness.

But because I have seen, again and again, that ordinary people can create extraordinary change.

Hope is not a feeling to me. It's an active discipline.

It's a decision to act when it would be easier to scroll, to care when it would be safer not to, to build when other people are busy tearing things down.

And privately? I would rather be the person holding a bucket of water than the one describing the fire.

Private Action

This is why, even when government systems feel destabilizing, frozen, and headlines feel hopeless, I still believe so deeply in entrepreneurs, philanthropists, and private action.

Because when the world gets messy, it's often not governments that show up first.

It's individuals.

It's the people who don't wait for permission, who see a problem and roll up their sleeves.

Whether it's:

- A nonprofit drilling wells in a village that doesn't exist on the map.
- A startup making healthcare affordable using AI, telemedicine, and a smartphone.
- A philanthropist quietly funding schools, clinics, or trauma care for refugees.
- A small business that pays fair wages to artisans and keeps ancient crafts alive.

Private innovation and compassionate capitalism have changed the world more than speeches or slogans ever could.

Here are just a few of my heroes:

- Scott Neeson, a former Hollywood executive, left the film industry to live in Phnom Penh's Steung Meanchey district and to build the Cambodian Children's Fund. He traded red carpets for dirt floors and has since provided education, healthcare, housing, and hope to over 2,800 children and their families, transforming the trajectory of an entire district of the country.
- Dr. Geoff Tabin and the Cure Blindness Project. For about $25 and 10 minutes of surgery, they restore sight

to people blinded by cataracts in remote mountain villages. Over 1.2 million people have regained their sight as a result of this effort.

- Yotam Polizer and IsraAID. Whether it's a war, earthquake, or a refugee crisis, IsraAID is one of the first on the ground. They don't just hand out supplies; they build water systems, train trauma counselors, restart schools, and stay long after the cameras leave. The work they do around the world is true Humanitarian Diplomacy.

These people don't just talk about change; they create it. They don't wait for systems to shift; they become the system.

That's why I believe in the private sector.

Not the greedy stereotype, but social impact innovation as a tool for problem-solving, wealth distribution, dignity of work, and real positive change. When rooted in ethics, generosity, and creativity, private enterprise and innovation become the most powerful forces for good on the planet.

It's not perfect.

But it works, especially when powered by people who care.

Teaching Hope to the Next Generation

As mothers, entrepreneurs, and leaders, many of us carry the same question in our hearts:

How do we raise children who are aware of the world's problems without being crushed by them?

How do we:

- Teach compassion without instilling fear?
- Encourage leadership without creating pressure?
- Show them the truth without stealing their optimism?

I've come to believe this:

Children don't need us to shield them from reality. They need us to show them how to use it.

They learn by watching how we react to hard things.

- When tragedy strikes, do we shut down, or do we show up?
- When the news feels overwhelming, do we sink into despair or choose action?
- When we see injustice, do we scroll past it or ask, "What can I do?"

For my family, hope was taught through experience, not lectures.

We took our kids to places where life looked very different from life in Mill Valley, California. Not to shock them, but to show them what resilience, gratitude, and human dignity look like in real life.

- In Zambia, they helped serve lunch to children at an AIDS orphanage.
- In Kenya's Maasai Mara, they helped mix mud and build walls for a rural classroom.
- In Ecuador's Amazon rainforest and India's Udaipur mountains, they saw what it looks like when a community builds something together with their hands, hearts, and hope.

- In Kakuma Refugee Camp, they played soccer with children who had lost everything except their joy.

This wasn't charity tourism; they were learning trips to better understand the needs of the communities and to fund a project that could help make lives a little bit better.

My sons didn't come home sad.
They came home aware.
And with awareness came responsibility.

They learned:

- The world is broken in places, but people are fixing it.
- You don't have to solve everything; you just have to start somewhere.
- Empathy isn't a feeling; it's a decision to act.

Because that's the truth I want my children, and yours, to know:

The world is full of problems. But it is also full of problem solvers.

Business as a Force for Good

One of the greatest lessons Serena & Lily taught me is this: business isn't just about profit; it's a platform—a platform for values and for impact. For how you treat people, make decisions, and leave your mark on the world.

We didn't build a "perfect" company, but we tried to make thoughtful decisions:

- We paid fairly and expected fairness from our partners.

- We created family-friendly policies because we were moms ourselves.
- We partnered with artisans, not as a charity play, but because beauty, craft, and economic dignity belong in business.
- And we always believed design could elevate life, not just decorate it.

That's when I realized something important:

Capitalism is only as good as the people who run it.
It can be extractive or generative.
It can take from the world or build for it.

Every brand, every founder, every entrepreneur gets to decide:
Does my company just make money?
Or
Does it make something better for employees, customers, communities, or the planet?

Even the smallest decisions matter:

- Who you hire
- Where you manufacture
- How you treat your team when times get tough
- Whether you design with longevity instead of landfills in mind
- Whether success means "me first" or "we together."

Your business doesn't need to solve world peace. It just needs to leave things a little better for one person, one supplier, one employee, or one community.

Because business isn't neutral.

It either contributes to the problem...

or becomes part of the solution.

In a Nutshell

Yes, the world often feels like it's on fire.

But I've come to believe this: hope is not a mood; it's a discipline.

Being hopeful doesn't mean ignoring reality. It means:

- You see things as they are...
- And still choose to imagine what they could be.

Hope is choosing action instead of apathy.
It's the entrepreneur launching something better.
It's the parent showing up, tired but present.
It's the ordinary person who says, "Someone should do something," and realizes... "I am someone."

The world will always give us reasons to feel helpless.
But it will also keep giving us people who build, repair, serve, protect, teach, create, and love in the middle of it all.

That's why I call myself a hope-a-holic.
Not because things are easy.
But because people, at their best, are extraordinary. And I want my kids, your kids, the next generation, to grow up not just being aware of the world's problems...
but convinced they can *do something* about them.

Reflection Questions

Take these to your journal, your team meeting, your family dinner table, or wherever honest conversations happen:

- How do you stay informed about the world without becoming overwhelmed or cynical?
- What gives you hope right now?
- Where in your life or business can you create positive change, no matter how small?
- What do your children (or the young people in your life) see you do when the world feels heavy?
- How can your business, career, or creative work solve a real problem—not just make a profit?
- When did you choose action over despair? What did it teach you?
- If you considered yourself a "hope-a-holic," what would that look like in practice, today, this week, this year?

CHAPTER 14

Building a Legacy of Purpose

The first time I saw those haunting photographs of kids living on top of a garbage landfill just outside Phnom Penh, Cambodia, I was shocked by the reality of it all.

Families were making a living by digging through mountains of trash, barefoot, with toxic smoke and dust swirling all around them, searching for anything they could sell to get by. And the worst part was that the kids were right there alongside them also digging, missing out on school because, let's be honest, survival takes priority.

You can't really comprehend the depth of it all until you see it for yourself, though, the kids playing and laughing in the same place where garbage trucks dump their loads. The smell, the smoke, the danger, and yet life just keeps on going, because it's just got to.

It was years ago that Scott Neeson stumbled upon this dump while traveling through Cambodia on a brief break between executive jobs in Hollywood. What he saw there changed him forever. Instead of just moving on, he was compelled to return and started doing what he could to get a few kids some education and a safe place to live.

Just that one decision to help out. Just one small beginning.

Today, thousands (2800+) of kids have gone through Cambodian Children's Fund programs and received a proper education, healthcare, and a chance at a life beyond poverty. What gets me is that it's not just the scale of the work; it's that reminder that real change often starts with just one person deciding they can't turn a blind eye. Many of the students have gone on to become Ph.D.s, and it's truly mind-blowing when you witness the possibility of the transformation of the human condition.

Scott Neeson with one of the most adorable children
we've had the complete pleasure to sponsor.

That experience has really stuck with me.

I think the thing that's stuck with me most about legacy is that it's not always something grand. Sometimes it starts with just deciding that saving one life actually matters.

As I've gotten older, one question's been nagging at me more and more:

What do we really leave behind, anyway?

When we're young, legacy feels like this abstract thing that's just not really relevant to our day-to-day lives. We're too busy building careers, raising families, paying the mortgage, chasing our goals. Legacy feels like something just about famous people or billionaires who end up having buildings named after them.

But the truth is that legacy isn't something we build at the end of our lives. It's what we do every day; it basically boils down to how we treat others on a daily basis.

And it's not just about the money. In fact, money's usually pretty close to the bottom of the list.

Some people have the means to give generously. Others have time, skills, networks, or just a willingness to help out. Some people mentor, some people volunteer, some people cook meals for their neighbors who are going through a tough time. Some people show up when life gets crazy and your friends need support. Some people write checks. All of it counts.

What matters most is that giving back is deeply personal; there's no one-size-fits-all approach. What moves one person might not move another.

Over time, though, I realized I needed some kind of framework for my own giving. Otherwise, I was just reacting to whatever crisis or fundraiser popped up that week. Every single cause out there is worthy, and there are just so many needs to be met. Without intention, giving becomes a reactionary thing instead of something that really means something.

So I started building a personal framework, hoping it might help others think about their own giving.

Not as a set of strict rules, just as a guide.

Pillar One: Identity and Community

My Jewish upbringing means a lot to me, not so much because of strict religious practice, but because of belonging to a peoplehood grounded in strong traditions, community, and the responsibility of passing culture from one generation to the next. It's a way of life with beautiful traditions that mark life's milestones.

I feel a deep connection to this civilization and a responsibility to help keep it alive for generations to come.

Today, Jewish people make up about 0.2% (.2 of 1%) of the world's population. Before World War II, that number was closer to 0.75%. Entire communities were wiped out, and even after all these decades, the population has never fully recovered.

For me, supporting a strong Jewish community culturally, educationally, and communally, feels both personal and necessary. It's about ensuring these traditions continue for future generations.

So a significant portion of my time and resources goes to that.

Not because others need to do the same, but because we should all do our part to protect what we care about most and what brings meaning to our lives.

Pillar Two: Investing in Women

One of my core principles is a commitment to women and girls; it always resonates with me. I still vividly remember hearing Cokie Roberts speak about why she was involved with Save the Children, the conviction in her voice as she explained the power of education for girls. She made a point that really stuck: when you educate girls, you don't just change their lives, you fundamentally shift the course of a country's history. She pointed out the example that South Korea was very poor back in the 1950s, but they made a huge bet on universal education for everyone, with girls included, and it paid off in a big way, helping the country grow into one of the world's leading economies in just a generation. Vietnam followed a similar path; it's been roughly 30 years since they made a major investment in education for everyone, including girls, and the results have been staggering. Poverty levels have plummeted from about 70% to under 6% now.

When girls get an education, they become way more likely to be in leadership, and they're more likely to bring other women with them on that journey. Educated girls tend to be part of healthier, more stable families, and that has a positive ripple effect on the community at large. Countries where women are represented in government tend to be less corrupt and invest way more in education, healthcare, and can attract foreign investment.

At the present moment in the United States, I find myself increasingly concerned about the possibility of the clock winding backward on women's rights to make decisions about their own bodies. Supporting women means supporting their ability to make deeply personal choices about their own lives and futures.

EmpowerHer is deeply personal to me because, despite women founding extraordinary companies, female-only founding teams still receive only about 2–3% of all venture capital funding. That gap isn't about talent or ambition; it's about access to capital and networks. Through EmpowerHer, we're working to change that by backing women with aligned capital, so more women can build companies that make a positive difference in the world.

Pillar Three: Global Humanity

My third pillar of giving is humanitarian work.

Travel has a way of opening your eyes to just how big the gap is between the haves and the have-nots. Once you've met families living in refugee camps or communities trying to rebuild after a disaster, it becomes pretty impossible to look away.

Some of the most inspiring work I've seen comes from organizations that fly under the radar, but are quietly making a difference in some of the toughest places on earth.

Our family made a commitment to Scott Neeson and the Cambodian Children's Fund because of the incredible impact they're having. When you see real transformation happening firsthand, it changes how you think about long-term giving.

This pillar also ties into my own work through Woven for Purpose and humanitarian partnerships like IsraAid; these efforts don't just aim to provide aid, but to give people the dignity and economic opportunity to change their own lives.

The older I get, the more I realize that charity alone just isn't enough. Opportunity and self-sufficiency are what really change lives.

Pillar Four: The People Right in Your Backyard

The final pillar of my giving is supporting the local community.

It's way too easy to focus on problems somewhere else, but the truth is that real impact often starts right where you live, supporting your neighbors, schools, workforce programs, and families who are just a short drive from your front door.

I'm currently focused on building a local giving circle. I'm bringing together my local community to pool our resources and make some real impact where we live.

Giving together multiplies not just money but also people's involvement, and it helps build a community among us givers. It's a great way to be in community and to make a greater impact.

Making Your Own Game Plan

None of these pillars are some kind of rulebook. They're more like the way I've learned to break down my giving so it aligns with my values over time. I don't by any means stick to these pillars 100%, but at least it helps me stay somewhat focused.

Your pillars might end up looking nothing like mine.

Maybe the thing that gets you most fired up is reproductive rights, supporting seniors, helping people with their mental health, investing in education, the arts, animal welfare, or medical research.

It's not even about which cause you care about; it's about choosing to put some thought into it.

Because your legacy isn't measured by how much money you've accumulated, but by the lives you've actually touched.

And your legacy isn't something you think about for the first time until the end of your life; it's something you build one choice at a time over years and decades.

I've come to believe that our sense of purpose really does change over time. At first, you're building, then you start thinking about how what you have built can be used to help others.

And maybe the real test of success is whether or not your life has made a little bit of a difference to people you've never even met.

Money is spent, businesses change hands, and job titles come and go.

But the good that you do in people's lives, that's what keeps on going way after you're gone.

And that, for me, is the kind of legacy I want to leave behind.

Because sometimes all it takes to change someone's life for the better is for you to decide not to just look away.

CHAPTER 15

Threads That Lead Us Home

Ever since meeting Serena, textiles have followed me everywhere.

At first, I didn't fully understand why. I just knew I was drawn to them. Markets, villages, tiny artisan stalls, wherever I traveled, I found myself running my fingers across woven fabrics, embroidered panels, hand-dyed cloth. I began bringing pieces home, layering them into our spaces, collecting them without quite knowing what story they were telling me.

But over time, I realized it wasn't just about design.

It was about people.

Each textile held history, identity, survival, and pride. These weren't just decorative objects — they were languages stitched into cloth.

I became obsessed.

Otomi embroidery from Mexico, alive with animals and mythology stitched in bold color. Ikat, like the patterns shown on the cover of this book from Uzbekistan, with designs that feel like motion captured in thread. Kuba cloth from Central Africa, woven in intricate geometric patterns that signal identity and status. Traditional block prints from India, where hand-carved wooden blocks stamp rhythmic, repeating motifs onto cloth. Suzani textiles from Central Asia, richly embroidered with suns, vines, and pomegranates symbolizing life and prosperity. Palestinian and Syrian embroidery, each village carrying its own pattern like a fingerprint passed from mother to daughter. Kanga cloth across East Africa, bright fabrics often carrying proverbs and messages printed directly into the cloth. Mud cloth from Mali, dyed with fermented mud using symbols that carry stories and social meaning. Indigo textiles, dyed through ancient processes perfected across West Africa, India, and Japan. Guatemalan huipil textiles, handwoven by Maya women with vibrant motifs that reflect village identity, cosmology, and everyday life. Japanese shibori, cloth shaped through intricate folding, binding, and stitching before dyeing to create organic patterns where no two pieces are ever the same. Berber textiles of North Africa, woven by Amazigh artisans into bold geometric forms that carry protective symbols and stories of home and tribe. Hmong embroidery from Southeast Asia, intricate stitched and appliqué textiles that often tell stories of migration, nature, and community through vivid color and pattern.

And the list kept growing.

Every piece held the fingerprints of women whose names we would never know—women supporting families, preserving culture, passing skills across generations, often in places where economic opportunity is scarce.

The more I learned, the harder it became to see textiles as just décor. These were livelihoods. These were survival tools. These were cultural memories.

And I began to wonder:

What if these traditions didn't just survive? What if they thrived?

What if global design could create economic opportunity while preserving cultural heritage? What if we could connect modern homes with ancient craft in a way that honored both?

The question slowly became an obsession:

How do we weave purpose into beauty?

And slowly, fascination turned into responsibility.

The more I learned about these textile traditions, the more I understood how fragile many of them are. Younger generations often leave villages in search of opportunity. Markets disappear. Middlemen capture most of the value. And in places already facing economic hardship or displacement, craft traditions are sometimes the only livelihood women can carry with them.

I kept asking myself: What if design could do more than decorate homes? What if it could help communities thrive?

And that question is leading me into my next adventure.

I'm now working to build a platform dedicated to global textiles, one that connects artisans in remote communities around the world to modern markets in a way that is dignified, sustainable, and economically meaningful. A platform that doesn't just sell beautiful things, but builds lasting income streams for the women and families who create them.

In many parts of the world, particularly in refugee camps and displaced communities, traditional craft skills are one of the few assets people can carry with them. Land is lost. Businesses disappear. Homes are destroyed. But the knowledge of how to weave, embroider, dye, or stitch travels in memory and hands.

If we can create reliable markets for these crafts, we can help provide something deeper than aid: income, independence, and dignity.

My hope is to build bridges between homes that want beauty and communities that need opportunity, weaving commerce and compassion together in a way that honors culture rather than exploiting it.

And when I step back, I can see how every chapter of my life has quietly prepared me for this one. Building a home brand taught me how people live with decorative objects. Entrepreneurship taught me how to build a brand and a channel of distribution. Philanthropy taught me how deep the need really is. And motherhood taught me that the world we leave behind matters more than the success we accumulate.

For so many years, my work was about creating beautiful homes. Now, it feels like the work is about helping create stability and opportunity in the homes of others.

This next chapter isn't about scale or valuation or exits. It's about impact. About preserving craft traditions. About giving women in remote villages and refugee camps a chance to support their families through skills they already possess.

It feels less like starting something new and more like coming home to something that has been calling me for years.

Threads connect us in ways we don't always see, across borders, cultures, and lives. A textile made in one corner of the world can end up on a sofa thousands of miles away, quietly carrying with it the story of the hands that made it.

If we do this right, those threads won't just carry beauty. They'll carry the opportunity to raise others.

And perhaps that is the real work now, not just weaving textiles, but weaving a little more dignity, connection, and hope into the fabric of our shared world.

This is the next adventure.

And I have a feeling it's the most meaningful one yet.

Conclusion

"The best time to plant a tree was 20 years ago. The second-best time is now."
—Chinese Proverb

My cell phone buzzed at 5:47 a.m. Our website pricing had gone haywire; a deleted cell in a spreadsheet meant certain products were selling for 5% of their actual price, and the internet was making it go viral. As I slipped out of bed to handle what could turn into a 6-figure disaster, I glanced at my sleeping husband, Marc. In a few hours, he'd be making breakfast, doing school drop-offs, and holding our family rhythm together while I tried to stop whatever fire was burning at work.

That moment, a business crisis on one side, family life quietly unfolding on the other—is everything this book is about.

Building a company and raising a family isn't about a perfect balance. It's about building systems, partnerships, humor, and values strong enough to survive the chaos. My story might be about growing a business, but the lessons apply whether you're running a startup, a household, a team, or simply trying to build a life that makes sense.

The Path We've Traveled Together

When we started, you might have believed what I once did, that the only way to "have it all" was to do it all, perfectly, all the time.

But life proved otherwise.

You saw how 13 years in corporate America became the training ground for entrepreneurship, even the jobs that seemed irrelevant at the time. Negotiating Microsoft retail leases became perfect practice for negotiating with textile suppliers in L.A. Handling egos at The O.P. Club helped prepare me for investor boardrooms years later.

You saw how the right life partner changes everything. Marc's support gave me the freedom to chase funding, travel for work, and put out fires, knowing our kids were safe, fed, and loved. And how meeting Serena in what could have been just another day at the store became the partnership that changed everything.

We didn't know what we were doing. But we did it anyway.

What You Now Know

Work-life balance isn't real. But being present is.

You learned it's not about splitting your time evenly; it's about being fully there when you are there. Family dinners mattered. Safari trips bonded us more than school drop-offs would have.

Capital can be a blessing and a nightmare.

You saw our "17-day miracle" raising $1.5 million, and the investor who patted us on the head and called us "girls" before offering millions. You learned that saying no can save your company just as much as saying yes.

You Can Grow Without Selling Your Soul

Serena & Lily became a heritage brand, not because we chased valuations, but because we refused to compromise on people, purpose, or product. We were never building to chase the next valuation. We were building to last.

Motherhood isn't the enemy of entrepreneurship. It's secret training.

If you can manage a colicky baby, negotiate with a toddler, and survive a Trader Joe's run with three kids under four, you're ready for venture capitalists, production delays, and shipping crises.

Leadership doesn't mean doing it all.

It means finding people better than you in certain things, giving them space to shine, and building a culture where people feel they belong.

And Now, the Next Chapter

As you've just read, my growing connection to global textile traditions has led me toward work that feels less about building brands and more about building bridges connecting communities that create beauty with markets that can help sustain them.

And it feels less like starting something new and more like answering something that has been calling me for a very long time.

Reflection Questions

- What is the "tree" you wish you had planted 20 years ago, and what is stopping you from planting it today?
- What problems in your life or in the world frustrate you the most, and could those actually be opportunities only you are meant to solve?
- Where are you waiting for permission, resources, or the "perfect moment," and what small step could you take today without any of those things?
- Who are the people in your life who have stood by you like Marc did for me? How can you honor, thank, or lean on them more intentionally?
- If your children (or the people you love most) were asked in 20 years what mattered to you, what would you hope they say? Does your daily life reflect that answer?
- In your work or business, where have you compromised out of fear, and where have you stood firm on your values? What did each of those choices cost or create?
- What is one boundary you need to set, one system you need to build, or one conversation you need to have so your life aligns more with your priorities?
- What parts of your life are you trying to perfect when they simply need presence, not perfection?
- What is the legacy you want to leave, not in revenue or titles, but in people, values, or impact?

Resources

Anti-Defamation League. (2024, April 16). U.S. antisemitic incidents soared 140 percent in 2023 – breaking all previous records [Press release]. https://www.adl.org/resources/press-release/us-antisemitic-incidents-soared-140-percent-2023-breaking-all-previous

Anderson, J. (2020, April 1). The benefit of family mealtime [Audio podcast]. EdCast. Harvard Graduate School of Education. https://www.gse.harvard.edu/ideas/edcast/20/04/benefit-family-mealtime

Cambodian Children's Fund. (n.d.). About us. Idealist.org. https://www.idealist.org/en/nonprofit/ea1a72c2c3a449d4894239c1974159a9-cambodian-childrens-fund-phnom-penh

Cure Blindness Project. (2025, May 28). Then & now: Types of blindness we treat. https://cureblindness.org/news/then-now-types-of-blindness-we-treat

FAO, IFAD and WFP. 2015. The State of Food Insecurity in the World 2015. Meeting the 2015 international hunger targets: taking stock of uneven progress. Rome, FAO.

Forman, H. P. (2024, October 11). Celebrating a milestone in the campaign to eliminate a major cause of blindness. Yale Insights. https://insights.som.yale.edu/insights/celebrating-milestone-in-the-campaign-to-eliminate-major-cause-of-blindness

Guterres, A. (2023, June 21). People in need of humanitarian assistance at record levels, Secretary-General tells Economic and Social Council, urging more aid funding, efforts to resolve conflict [Press release]. United Nations. https://press.un.org/en/2023/sgsm21852.doc.htm

Hinchliffe, E. (2024, June 4). The share of Fortune 500 companies run by women CEOs stays flat at 10.4% as pace of change stalls. Fortune. https://fortune.com/2024/06/04/fortune-500-companies-women-ceos-2024/

Hutton, G., & Chase, C. (2017). Water supply, sanitation, and hygiene. In Injury prevention and environmental health (3rd ed., Chapter 9). The World Bank. https://www.ncbi.nlm.nih.gov/books/NBK525207/

Lemon, J. (2021, June 25). Majority of Gen Z Americans hold negative views of capitalism: Poll. Newsweek. https://www.newsweek.com/majority-gen-z-americans-hold-negative-views-capitalism-poll-1604334

Polizer, Y. (2024, March). IsraAID: Meeting the needs in Israel requires all of our humanitarian experience. eJewish Philanthropy. Retrieved from https://koret.org/grantees/israaid-meeting-needs-israel-requires-humanitarian-experience/

Picchi, A. (2023, August 31). More than 60% of Americans are living paycheck to paycheck. Here's what researchers say is to blame. CBS News. https://www.cbsnews.com/news/paycheck-to-paycheck-6-in-10-americans-lendingclub/

Roser, M., & Ortiz-Ospina, E. (2018). Literacy. Our World in Data. https://ourworldindata.org/literacy

Simons, B. (2025, February 19). Why the crisis in global aid is bigger than Trump. ODI Global. https://odi.org/en/insights/why-the-crisis-in-global-aid-is-bigger-than-trump/Retry

St. Aubin, C., & Liedke, J. (2024, September 17). Social media and news fact sheet. *Pew Research Center*. https://www.pewresearch.org/journalism/fact-sheet/social-media-and-news-fact-sheet/

UNICEF. (2025, March). Under-five mortality. UNICEF Data: Monitoring the situation of children and women. https://data.unicef.org/topic/child-survival/under-five-mortality/

UN Women. (2024). Women's economic empowerment strategy. UN Women.

Walton, A. G. (2017, July 10). The science of giving back: How having a purpose is good for body and brain. Forbes. https://www.forbes.com/sites/alicegwalton/2017/07/10/the-science-of-giving-back-how-having-a-purpose-is-good-for-body-and-brain/

Center for Disease Control (2024, September 29). 2023 Youth Risk Behavior Survey Results. 2023 Youth Risk Behavior Survey Results | Youth Risk Behavior Surveillance System (YRBSS) | CDC

PYMNTS Intelligence (2026, January 29) Reality Check: Paycheck-to-Paycheck Research series.

https://www.pymnts.com/study_posts/tax-refund-season-reveals-the-reality-of-paycheck-to-paycheck-america/#first_title

Pew Research Center (2025, April 22) Teens, Social Media and Mental Health. Social Media and Teens' Mental Health: What Teens and Their Parents Say | Pew Research Center

Anti-Defamation League (2025, April 22) Audit of Antisemitic Incidents 2024. Audit of Antisemitic Incidents 2024 | ADL

www.ingramcontent.com/pod-product-compliance
Lightning Source LLC
Chambersburg PA
CBHW051152130726
47988CB00005B/2090